THYME AND THE RIVER

Recipes from Oregon's Steamboat Inn

THYME AND THE RIVER

Recipes
from Oregon's
Steamboat Inn

by Sharon Van Loan and Patricia Lee
With Mark Hoy

Sharon H Van Loan

Patricia A Lee

GRAPHIC ARTS CENTER PUBLISHING COMPANY

Portland, Oregon

International Standard Book Number 0-932575-67-6

Library of Congress Catalog Number 88-80475

Copyright ©1988 Graphic Arts Center Publishing Company

P.O. Box 10306 • Portland, Oregon 97210 • 503/226-2402

Scenic photography ©1988 Dan Callaghan

Food photography ©1988 E. J. Carr

Drawings ©1988 John and Judy Waller

Editor-in-Chief • Douglas A. Pfeiffer

Designer • Marra/Dean Associates

Typographer • Harrison Typesetting, Inc.

Printer • Graphic Arts Center

Bindery • Lincoln & Allen

Printed in the United States of America

Frontispiece: The Boat Pool Crossing

Contents

We love to surprise our guests at the Steamboat Inn. After all, when you've cooked together almost every day for over a decade, as we have, the chances of surprising each other are pretty slim. The recipes found in this cookbook are our accumulated experiments—our surprises—and are the product of a culinary collaboration that results each evening in the event known as the Fisherman's Dinner.

These recipes, even our old favorites, have been tested over and over again until we feel we've refined each one to suit our tastes. Even then, sometimes we will experiment again with a dish on a whim—just so we can sample the results. Of course, our experiments aren't random. Over the years, we've sharpened our senses and learned from our mistakes.

One of the reasons our guests return year after year to visit us at the Steamboat Inn is the sense of adventure we share with them. No two days spent on the North Umpqua River are ever quite the same. Some days are filled with activity—hiking, fishing, or swimming. Sometimes the big steelhead are biting, and the fly-fishing is fast and furious. Then there are days when it's better to just sit and watch the river flow.

That's how we feel about our cooking, too. Some days are perfect for fussing over one of our sauces, trying to find the ultimate blend of seasonings. At other times, we feel more like concocting the most elegant of desserts. When the mood strikes to try something different, we like to let it carry us away!

Variety is important to us, too. It's the key ingredient in keeping the cooks interested and the food exciting. Like days spent on the river, no two Fisherman's Dinners are ever quite the same. Our guests come to visit from all over the world—and with so many different people and diverse backgrounds, we have to work hard to match all that variety with our evening meals. One of our "secrets" is to keep records of the meals we've served our regular guests in years past. Then we try to ensure that their sense of adventure will be challenged by unique combinations of food when they visit us again. Unless, of course, they request an old-favorite recipe during their stay.

We feel lucky to live in the Northwest, with its bountiful variety of fresh foods from farmlands, rivers, and the ocean. We love to think of new ways to serve fresh lamb in season or feature fresh salmon in the meal when the fish are running. Lots of people in our area grow big gardens, so we never have to worry about getting the freshest vegetables in the summer—or the rest of the year—in our mild climate. Although many of our recipe ingredients are indigenous to the Northwest, most are also readily available in other regions of the country.

Recently, we've noticed a new interest in variety and creativity in preparing the fresh foods from our region. Some people even say there's a new Northwest cuisine in the making. We couldn't be more pleased with that idea, because it fits in so perfectly with what we've been doing in the kitchen at Steamboat Inn for the past decade. We'd like to believe that the Steamboat Inn incorporates the best of both the traditional fishing camp cooking along the river and the new, healthy approaches to preparing fresh foods.

Finally, we would like this volume to be a "working cookbook," one that inspires to new heights of cooking pleasure without intimidating its user with formulas and pat answers. We hope the recipes we have put together will be useful to the novice cook as an introduction to fine cuisine, and also provide a new point of departure for cooks with more experience in handling food. If you see an opportunity to experiment with one of our tried-and-true recipes, by all means, go ahead! We've learned a great deal in the kitchen at the Steamboat Inn—but we've also learned from chefs in France, from pioneer women in the Umpqua Valley, and from our guests who wouldn't consider their visit to the Steamboat Inn complete without sharing their likes and dislikes with us.

And discover for yourself that sense of adventure we share in the kitchen! Much of our success at the Steamboat Inn stems from the principle that every meal should be treated with the same care and attention it would get in our own homes. Cooking with a sense of adventure and variety can be satisfying—like time spent at the river's edge. When you see the results of all this culinary fun, we think you'll be proud to serve your family and guests your own version of our Fisherman's Dinner.

Patricia Lee and Sharon Van Loan

By lantern light
the fishermen come
to the edge
of this rushing darkness,
where the fog sits
and the fish stir.
Everything is waiting
for morning.

◆

Sixty feet out on a spider line,
a small grey moth
dances above a feeding trout.
A dark swirl that misses.
A circus of floating line
above your head,
you cast again.

◆

Gravity is everywhere,
the mutiny of white water
fills our ears.
The sweet flowers
reach out and grab our eyes.
All beauty surrounds
our passing here.

◆

*Above the river
the afternoon gets lazy in its legs
and the light slants
in the dry straw air.
In the warm quiescent sun
we climb these winding stairs
of maple leaves
to comforts of a different sort.*

◆

THYME AND THE RIVER

And now this gentle snow
sits us down to fireplaces
of fractured light and shadow fish
that swim the windows.
We sleep in dreams of spring.
Look, the emerald river
is still here and the
flowering dogwoods begin to sing.

◆

Peter Coyne

A History
of the Steamboat Inn
& the Fly-Fishing Tradition
on the North Umpqua River

by Mark Hoy

The Steamboat Inn perches on a bluff above some of the best fishing water on the North Umpqua River, a cold, clear Cascades Range stream with a long and storied angling tradition. The upper stretches of the North Umpqua have been fished by fly anglers for more than half a century—and many of the anglers who came to test themselves against this formidable river were among the best fly-fishermen of their day.

In keeping with the wilderness fishing experience, the camp cooks at the old fishing camps along the North Umpqua outdid themselves to ensure that the angler's good fishing would be matched by the quality of the food they enjoyed. The Fisherman's Dinner served several important purposes. The anglers gathered around the dinner table each evening to exchange information on the flies and methods of presentation that had been successful on that day in luring the river's native summer steelhead to hand. In the process of rehashing the day's exploits, a camaraderie developed among these anglers that often helped forge life-long friendships.

These traditions are carried on today by Sharon Van Loan and Patricia Lee in the kitchen at the Steamboat Inn. Guests still gather around the long sugar pine table in the dining room to exchange fishing stories and strengthen old friendships—or begin new ones. And they enjoy a distinctive dinner cuisine that heightens their enjoyment of the river experience.

But many of today's guests know little of the history of fly-fishing on the North Umpqua or the important role the Steamboat Inn and its predecessor fishing camps played in promoting that tradition. This chapter is an effort to gather reminiscences of an earlier generation of fly-fishermen and the scattered written accounts of the pioneering days along the North Umpqua River. We hope it will help you to gain a deeper appreciation of the Fisherman's Dinner, the Steamboat Inn, and the river itself.

Early Fishing Camps

The earliest sport fishing camps were established in the Steamboat area in the 1920s. Prior to that time, a rough trail provided the only access to the area. After the native peoples had left the area in the late nineteenth century, the only visitors were a few hardy homesteaders, some prospectors looking for gold, and hunters in search of deer and elk.

The gold miners probably provided the name "Steamboat" for the creek that enters the main river near the present site of the Inn. Although a rich deposit of gold was discovered in a nearby drainage—later named the Bohemia Mining District—Steamboat Creek was prospected extensively without yielding similar results. In the miners' parlance of the day, if an area did not come up to expectations, or claims had been fraudulently sold to unsuspecting newcomers, the miners leaving the scene were said to have "steamboated" out of the area. No one knows who first applied the term to Steamboat Creek, but the name was in general use by the 1890s.

Much to the disappointment of many first-time visitors to the area, there is no evidence that any steamboat ever navigated the upper stretches of the North Umpqua. Even a cursory look at the river in this area—filled with large boulders and sections of foaming whitewater—confirms the fact that modern jet boats, which can run upstream in as little as six inches of water, could scarcely make the passage, let alone a wood-bottomed steamboat.

A dirt road, blazed high on the canyon wall above the river, was completed all the way upriver to Steamboat in 1927. Although the trip was slow and sometimes treacherous, anglers began to transport their gear by motorized trucks or cars to the junction of Steamboat Creek and the North Umpqua River, where they established summer fishing camps.

These anglers were attracted to the area by stories of heavy runs of summer steelhead, a type of rainbow trout that spawns in freshwater but descends certain rivers to the ocean. There the steelhead spend two to five years feeding and growing and then return to their native streams to spawn. Unlike salmon, many steelhead live on after spawning. They return to the ocean and, occasionally, return upstream for a second time to spawn.

In the early days, the North Umpqua also supported strong runs of Chinook and Coho salmon, as well as sea-run cutthroat trout. Today, development has reduced these species, except for the spring Chinook salmon, to remnant runs. However, aided by hatchery-spawned fish, the runs of summer steelhead remain comparable to, and in some years exceed, the numbers of fish found in the river by the first fly anglers.

The fishermen discovered that a few hardy souls had preceded them. A recluse named "Umpqua" Vic O'Byrne had established a camp a few miles upstream from Steamboat, across the river from an old, abandoned fish hatchery. The spot was known as Hatchery Ford, because it was one of the few places where a pack train of horses and mules could cross the river. O'Byrne built a cabin and fished for salmon and steelhead in grand solitude. He was reputed to have been a military man before he "took to the wilds." He later drowned in what some considered mysterious circumstances, since his glasses and other personal effects were found laid out neatly on his cabin table after his body was recovered from the river downstream.

Farther upstream, Perry and Jessie Wright had proved up a homestead at Illahee Flats in 1915.

For many years, the Wrights packed in supplies with horses and mules for the Forest Service and early hunters in the area. Jessie Wright, now almost ninety years old, has written an entertaining account of the pioneer days on the North Umpqua, titled *How High the Bounty*.

The first sports angler of national reputation to adopt the North Umpqua was Major Jordan Lawrence Mott who first arrived in the Steamboat area in 1929. He established a summer fishing camp on the south side of the main river, opposite the junction of Steamboat Creek and the North Umpqua. His camp surveyed the series of fishing pools that would later become known collectively as "the camp water." Because many of the native summer steelhead in the North Umpqua spawn in Steamboat Creek and remain in the main river until the first heavy rains of the fall season allow them to enter the creek, this area was (and remains) one of the most productive fishing areas on the entire river.

Major Lawrence Mott

Before he came to Steamboat, Major Mott led a life straight out of a romantic novel. When Mott was born in New York in 1881, his father was the president of J. L. Mott Iron Works and reputedly controlled a fortune in excess of $25 million. The younger Mott graduated from Harvard and went to work as a reporter in New York City. However, he covered his assignments in a chauffeur-driven, imported limousine and was dubbed the "millionaire reporter."

Unhappy in his first marriage, Mott fell in love with a married woman, Frances Hewitt Bowne. They eloped to Europe on a tramp steamer in 1912—scandalous behavior for the time since neither of the young lovers had bothered to secure a divorce. Mott's father hired another New York newspaperman, Hector Fuller, to track them down. Fuller pursued the happy couple across several continents before finally locating them in Hong Kong, where Mrs. Bowne was singing light opera to earn them a meager income. When Mott refused to return to New York City, his father promptly disinherited him.

During World War I, Mott served in the U. S. Army Signal Corps and was commissioned a major. After the war, the couple lived on Santa Catalina Island in California where Mott pursued deep-sea fishing for marlin and became prominent in the emerging radio industry. He also authored numerous magazine articles and books on the outdoors, including a successful novel entitled *Jules of the Great Love*. In 1928, after finally receiving their respective divorces, he and Frances were wed.

Much of Major Mott's time in his later years was spent campaigning for conservation of wildlife and natural resources. He was attracted to the North Umpqua for its excellent steelhead fishing and made his summer camp there until his premature death, at age 50, in 1931. Mott cherished his time at Steamboat so much that even after he had contracted the cancer that eventually killed him, he traveled from California to his camp at Steamboat to spend his final days on the river.

Major Mott's legacy is well preserved in the Steamboat area. The bridge leading from the main North Umpqua Highway across the river to the site of his old camp still bears his name, as do a series of nearby fishing pools, collectively known as "Mott Water." The fisherman's trail that provides access to the south bank of the North Umpqua River is now maintained by the Forest Service and officially known as the Mott Trail.

While still in camp at Steamboat, Major Mott hired a local man, Zeke Allen, to cook, do chores around camp, and guide him while he learned to fish the river. After Mott's death, Allen inherited most of the fishing and camping gear, as well as the use of Major Mott's campsite. Zeke Allen continued to guide the few anglers who came to fish for steelhead in the summer, as well as hunters who arrived in the fall to pursue deer and elk.

The same year that Major Mott first visited the North Umpqua, another nationally known sportsman, Captain Frank Winch, made a short visit to Steamboat. Winch, like Mott, had been told of the area by John Ewell, who operated a motel in nearby Roseburg and had rustic cabins near the junction of Steamboat Creek and Canton Creek. Winch was a field scout for *Forest and Stream Magazine* and an accomplished hunter and fisherman. He fished with Major Mott for only one evening but caught a seven-pound steelhead. As Winch later reported:

> I have been on every trout stream of importance in the entire northern part of the United States, but I have never seen a real trout stream until I fished in the North Umpqua River today. Words cannot possibly express my enthusiasm for your North Umpqua. I am still dizzy from the thrill. . . .

Zane Grey on the North Umpqua

The spring after Major Mott's death, in 1931, marked the appearance at Steamboat of perhaps the most famous sportsman in America, Zane Grey. During the last half of the 1920s, Grey had split his fishing time between ocean cruises to the South Seas in search of world record marlin and regular forays to fly-fish for summer steelhead on the Rogue River in southwestern Oregon. At least in part because of

Grey's own articles and books, the Rogue River became too crowded to suit Grey's taste. In June of 1932, he stopped to camp in the Steamboat area as a layover on his trip to Campbell River, British Columbia.

Grey's first camp was near the junction of Steamboat and Canton creeks. As was his custom, the camp was part business enterprise, part fishing extravaganza. On this trip, Grey was accompanied by his son, Romer, and his daughter-in-law, as well as a frequent fishing companion, Dr. J. A. Wiborn, and Wiborn's wife. In addition, Grey's secretaries were along (for help on his writing projects) and he rarely traveled without his loyal Japanese cook, George Takahashi, as well as several cameramen and other technicians who worked for Romer Grey Motion Picture Corporation.

Zane Grey tying on a fly

Merle Hargis, a Forest Service packer stationed at Steamboat, was asked by his boss to transport Grey's camp equipment up the hill to John Ewell's cabins. Hargis remembers that it took three trips with the six mules in his string to transport all the gear—eighteen loads in all! Afterwards, Zane Grey put his arm around Hargis, thanked him warmly, and gave the packer four half-dollars as a reward for his efforts.

Later that summer, Grey and his party moved their camp down to the point where Steamboat Creek enters the North Umpqua River. Across the river was Major Mott's old camp, now occupied by Zeke Allen and a few anglers he was guiding. They all fished the Camp Water, particularly the Plank Pool (now known as the Station Pool), which took its name from the boards which had been laid out from shore to a large rock. The old Forest Service Guard Station was across from Grey's camp, and the plank was used by one and all to secure water for washing and cooking, as well as a convenient platform for fishing the productive pool below.

When Grey camped on the North Umpqua, he was guided by Joe DeBernardi, a resident of the little community downstream known as Glide. That first summer, Romer Grey and his movie technicians constructed several wooden boats in camp, copying the design of boats being constructed at that time on the Rogue River by Glen Wooldridge. Romer convinced Joe DeBernardi to help pilot the boats downstream from Steamboat to Rock Creek while his camera crew filmed the white-water passage "to provide thrills for his motion picture audiences."

Apparently, the boaters got more of a thrill than they bargained for. According to a news account of the day, several of the boats were wrecked against rocks and "time and again the occupants of the boats were thrown out into the icy waters to battle swift currents for their lives." DeBernardi narrowly escaped death when the boat in which he and Romer Grey were riding was crushed against an overhanging ledge and an oarlock punctured DeBernardi's side. Fortunately, he managed to hang on to the overturned craft until it reached calmer water.

Thus, modern-day river running on the North Umpqua was born. Romer Grey reported that "the Umpqua provided him with more thrills and exciting experiences than any other water he has ever attempted." However, the Grey party repeated the thrilling adventure only one more time, and in subsequent seasons the boats were used primarily to ferry fishermen and guests across the river.

Zane Grey enjoyed his initial visit to the Steamboat area so much that he stayed on until the end of July, well beyond his intended departure date for Campbell River. After another winter cruise to New Zealand, Grey and his party returned to the North Umpqua in the summer of 1933 when they stayed at Zeke Allen's camp. Dissatisfied with Allen's unkempt campsite and some of his fishing methods, Grey moved his camp downstream in 1934 to Maple Ridge, the present site of the Steamboat Inn.

Interestingly, while there is a fishing pool near the Maple Ridge campsite named for Grey's cook, Takahashi, no landmarks on the North Umpqua today bear the name of the famous writer himself. During the 1930s, part of the Mott Water was called the ZG Pool for a time but later reverted to its old name. Grey is reputed to have named the Ledges Pool and several others in the area downstream from Steamboat.

Zane Grey preparing for his battles with marlin

The most convincing explanation for the lack of a river memorial to Grey seems to be that while ZG (as he was known) was respected for his power and reputation as a writer, he was not well-loved by other anglers or local residents. When Grey camped along a stretch of water, he considered the fishing pools to be his own private domain. Many old-timers on the North Umpqua still remember how ZG's assistants attempted to prevent them from fishing their favorite spots before the famous author arrived to cast his fly in the morning.

Then, as now, this high-handed behavior did not sit well with the local fly-fishermen. The gentleman's code on the North Umpqua dictated that the first angler to reach a fishing pool could fish through without interruption, providing he did not "hog" the area for an extended period of time. The same code still applies today.

Grey's dislike for the "crowded" fishing conditions at Steamboat probably explains his move downstream to the Williams Creek area in subsequent years. When Clarence Gordon took over the old Mott Camp and entertained a steady stream of well-to-do anglers from Southern California and the East Coast, Grey sought a more secluded fishing camp for his 1935 visit to the North Umpqua.

He found it across from Williams Creek, on the south side of the river. All equipment and visitors had to be ferried across by boat, so Grey was able to control access and maintain his distance from other anglers. His camp was reported to be one of the cleanest and best organized ever seen on the North Umpqua. He even brought the heavy seat and rod apparatus that he used in marlin fishing, so he could practice straining against weights for thirty minutes daily to stay in shape for his battles with marlin that could weigh over a thousand pounds.

Grey's party enjoyed some fabulous fly-fishing for summer steelhead during their visits to the North Umpqua. They found that the steelhead were bigger than the fish they had become accustomed to on the Rogue. On the Umpqua, the steelhead averaged six to eight pounds and could sometimes weigh in at as much as fifteen pounds. Loren, Grey's youngest son, had joined

the party in 1934 and the next summer he reported catching over one hundred steelhead in less than two months of fishing. Others reported similar totals.

However, Zane Grey became increasingly concerned about the future of the steelhead runs on the North Umpqua. He published just one article about it, hoping to shield the river from the publicity that he felt had ruined the Rogue. In that article he pleaded for wise management of the North Umpqua, decrying the practice by commercial fishermen of placing racks in the river to trap salmon—which incidentally killed thousands of steelhead. He also gave much-needed support to a delegation from the Roseburg Rod and Gun Club who appeared before the Oregon State Game Commission and succeeded in having Steamboat Creek, the river's prime spawning ground, closed to angling.

For a man in his sixties, Zane Grey kept himself in remarkable condition since he exercised regularly and never smoked or drank. Photos taken during his visits to the North Umpqua show a vigorous, tanned, and lean sportsman

A vigorous Zane Grey splitting wood in camp

with keen eyes and a distinctive shaggy mop of gray hair. Nevertheless, it was during Grey's North Umpqua visit of 1937 that he suffered the stroke which eventually led to his death in 1939. He never returned to his camp near Williams Creek, and another legendary figure on the North Umpqua passed from the scene.

Fred Burnham was another famous North Umpqua angler whose name is closely associated with Zane Grey's. Burnham married into money after his graduation from the University of California, and his job as a stock broker allowed him the leisure to fish all the famous salmon and steelhead rivers of his day. Standing over six feet three inches tall, he was a gifted athlete with ample strength and coordination. He owned property on the Rogue and his prowess there as a fly-fisherman was well known.

After Zane Grey's first visit to the Rogue in 1916, Burnham served as ZG's mentor in the art of fly casting for summer steelhead. Their styles were a study in contrasts. Burnham was the "natural," an acknowledged expert in the sport. Grey, himself a gifted athlete and a semipro baseball player in his youth, struggled as he learned to cast a fly line long distances and never quite achieved the grace that Burnham exhibited. In a sense, Grey was the victim of his self-created image as a record-holding angler. When he failed, he was forced to fall back on excuses, such as failing fish runs or simple bad luck. Burnham and Grey also fished together (or more precisely, in competition) for record-breaking marlin in the South Seas.

It was Burnham who first urged Zane Grey to try fishing the North Umpqua. During his early visits, Burnham stayed at the Circle H Ranch, downstream from Steamboat at Susan Creek. This small resort predated the camps at Steamboat since the road had reached the Susan Creek area at an earlier time. The Circle H resort also offered horseback riding and outfitted pack trips for hunters in the early days.

Burnham was well-known in the area as a skilled fly-fisherman, whose height and strength allowed him to wade areas of the river that lesser men could never dare to challenge. He later transferred his North Umpqua angling trips upstream to Steamboat, where he stayed at the new lodge constructed by Clarence Gordon.

Clarence Gordon at the tying vise

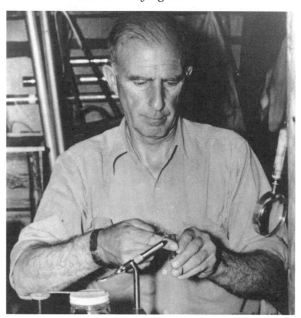

The North Umpqua Lodge

Like many others who were to make their impact on the fly-fishing scene along the North Umpqua, Clarence Gordon was introduced to the Steamboat area by John Ewell. In 1929, Gordon and his wife, Delia, stayed at Ewell's Camp View Motel in Roseburg on a trip from Southern California to Victoria, British Columbia. Ewell took Gordon upriver to sample the fishing at Steamboat, while Delia remained behind in Roseburg. Enchanted with the area, the Gordons stopped in again for a few days—camping in the Susan Creek area—on their return trip from Canada.

Gordon returned with a friend and his 15-year-old son on a fishing trip the next summer. The following year, 1931, he and Delia drove to Steamboat, where they left their car, and let Jessie and Perry Wright pack their gear to a camping spot on Dry Creek, about 10 miles up-river from Steamboat. It was on this trip that Gordon began to dream of operating a "mountain lodge or resort" on the "beautiful point across the river from the Ranger Station" at Steamboat. Of course, this was the old camp of Major Mott, who had died that spring, and the camp was now occupied by Zeke Allen.

By 1934, however, Gordon had secured the necessary approval from the Forest Service to set up a rustic resort on the old Major Mott campsite. By the summer of 1935, the "resort" consisted of several tents and a rustic dining room and kitchen near the water's edge. The Kitchen Pool on the river, famous among anglers, gained its name because the view from the kitchen tent looked directly out over the pool. Before the Mott Bridge was erected in the late 1930s, guests arriving on the north side of the river rang a bell there in order to alert someone in camp to row across and ferry them and their baggage to camp. Ever since, this section of the North Umpqua has been known as the Boat Pool.

Throughout this period, Gordon also managed the Smoke Tree Ranch in Palm Springs and a resort in Pasadena during the winter season. Using his contacts in Southern California, he began to attract a regular group of professional and other well-to-do men and their wives to his fishing camp which he called the North Umpqua Lodge. This regular clientele sustained the resort during the 1930s, when it became something of a haven for doctors, lawyers, and other professional men.

Some local residents, as well as some Forest Service employees who visited the lodge, thought the Gordons guilty of catering to an elite crowd. A price list for the 1938 season shows that the standard charges for an individual at the lodge were $3.50 a night for a cabin without a bath and $5.00 per night for a room with a bath, on the American Plan (meals included). Guide service cost $5.00 a day for two anglers.

Admitted one Forest Service official:
There is certainly no reason to complain about the accommodations, or, I believe, the prices charged. Although, I admit that $7.00 or $10.00 per day per couple is pretty high for the average individual, and it is entirely out of the question for people in the middle brackets of salary income to take the family to a resort of this type.

Clarence Gordon was considered a top angler and guide on the river in his day. He was a large, quiet man—intense in his own way—who could become quite a promoter when it came to the North Umpqua. He invited Ray Bergman, of Nyack, New York, the angling editor of *Outdoor Life* magazine, to come sample the fishing at his camp. Bergman and his wife, Grace, visited Steamboat and enjoyed the fishing and companionship so much that they returned the next year. Bergman's experiences resulted in several articles in *Outdoor Life*. In his classic book, *Trout*, he also included an entire chapter called "Steelheads of the Umpqua." Together, his writings give us a taste of life in the Gordon camp and a detailed portrait of the fly-fishing methods of the day.

Bergman's *Trout* also provides tying instructions for some of the most popular fly patterns in use on the North Umpqua in the 1930s. They included the Cummings (developed by guide Ward Cummings), the Umpqua, the Sawtooth, and the Surveyor—the latter two named after well-known fishing pools on the river. Not pictured in the book, but extensively used on the North Umpqua, was the Black Gordon, a pattern developed by Clarence Gordon. Some experts believe that the Skunk pattern—one of the most widely-used flies today for steelhead—was developed during this era on the North Umpqua, although its origins remain obscure.

During the 1930s, the Forest Service pressured Gordon to make his North Umpqua Lodge permanent by building additional cabins and a lodge on a bench above the high-water mark of the river. Eventually, the "dugout" was constructed, consisting of four bedrooms and baths, as well as a central living room. Later, more floored tents and cabins, an office building, and a fly-tying room were added.

The Fisherman's Dinner also began to take more definite form at the North Umpqua Lodge. A bachelor logger named Scott and a 16-year-old guide at the lodge, Knute Kershner, constructed the dining table and benches—hewn from large sugar pine logs—which are still in use today at the Steamboat Inn.

Delia Gordon, a graduate of the Julliard School of Music and a woman of culture, presided over dinner and was reputed to be an excellent cook. However, much of the cooking was done by hired camp cooks, beginning with Zeke Allen, who stayed on at the Gordon lodge for some years.

The dinners relied heavily on local fish and game, since foodstuffs came from Roseburg on the rough road to Steamboat. Grilled or smoked steelhead was, of course, a mainstay, as was venison. More than one cougar was shot in or near the camp, and bears were often hunted in the area, but there is no evidence that either was ever featured as an entrée in the evening meal. In many ways, the early camp fare relied on many of the foods that native peoples in the Umpqua Valley had exploited for centuries: native fish and game, local nuts and wild berries, and whatever could be coaxed from a garden during the summer growing season.

The Fisherman's Dinner acquired substantial new flair after the arrival of camp cooks Harry and Dolly Killeior. This couple had previously starred in vaudeville acts, and their sense of showmanship soon began to add a unique element to the evening meal. Harry reportedly did most of the cooking, with Dolly serving as his "straight man," as it were. From all accounts, they turned out superb meals that were well-appreciated by the guests.

However, the Killeiors also insisted that the dinner show must go on promptly—at seven o'clock each evening. This mandate posed a dilemma for the avid fly anglers in camp since the last hour before dark was usually the best time of day to lure summer steelhead to a fly. They were often forced to choose between eating and fishing—which sometimes resulted in grumbling anglers (as well as stomachs!) around camp.

Business was slow at the North Umpqua Lodge during the early 1940s, as the war effort took young men overseas and restricted travel for those left at home. After the war, business at the resort picked up briefly, only to be dashed by two monumental undertakings on the river—dam building and road construction.

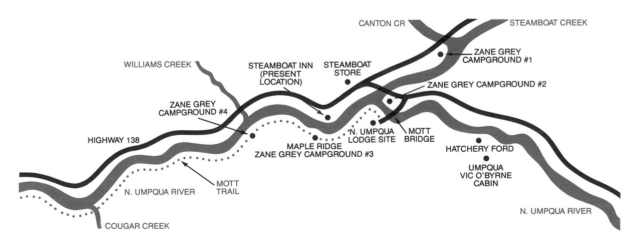

In the mid-1920s, the California Oregon Power Company (COPCO) surveyed the North Umpqua drainage for potential dam sites, with the goal of generating hydroelectric power. Seven sites were identified on the main river. Anglers and other sportsmen protested loudly that the two sites farthest downriver—one at Rock Creek and the other near the North Umpqua Forest boundary—would flood large sections of the canyon, destroy the fish runs and ruin any potential recreation development in the future. In response, COPCO agreed to begin its power development in the river's upper reaches, moving to sites farther downstream as demand dictated.

After World War II, dam building began in earnest upstream in the area near Toketee. Part of the development plan for the area also included a new road, to be built at river grade along the upper North Umpqua. The new road would complement dam construction, provide access for timber companies to vast tracts of old-growth forests, and also complete a high-speed highway between Diamond Lake and Roseburg.

The results of all this new development were disastrous for Gordon's North Umpqua Lodge and the river itself. Dam building resulted in heavy siltation and river levels that fluctuated wildly, dwindling away at times and then rising rapidly when flood gates were opened. The runs of summer steelhead were severely impacted—in some years, there was not enough water released at the appropriate times for the fish to return upstream from the ocean—and fishermen feared for their lives whenever they waded the river. Road building at river level introduced even more silt into the river, further damaging the fishing and steelhead spawning beds.

In 1951, in an effort to preserve the dwindling runs of salmon and steelhead, Clarence Gordon and members of the Roseburg Rod and Gun Club were instrumental in persuading the Oregon State Game Commission to change the regulations on the North Umpqua to "fishing with artificial flies only" in the area from Rock Creek all the way upstream to the new dams being built on the upper river.

In 1952, after the Gordons had already completed their reservation list for the summer season, the heavy dam-building activities made the river completely unfishable. They were forced to cancel all reservations. From 1952 until 1955, the lodge was closed, with only the Gordons' old friends visiting their camp.

The only bright spot was the Steamboat Store, a small lunch-counter operation which Clarence Gordon had opened near the junction of Steamboat Creek and the North Umpqua River. There the Gordons served hot lunches and operated a small store for the construction crews. Later, the store was moved to the present site of the Steamboat Inn, where the building which now houses the Inn's main dining room and kitchen was constructed by Gordon.

The North Umpqua Lodge buildings on the south side of the river were leased to a construction company to house their personnel during 1953 and 1954. In 1955, the Forest Service purchased Gordon's holdings on the south side of the river and moved the Steamboat Ranger Station to the site. This was the end of the old North Umpqua Lodge, but the Steamboat Store across the river would soon evolve and continue the area's fishing camp tradition.

Beginnings of the Steamboat Inn

Frank Moore first fished the North Umpqua in 1946. Before long, he was guiding for Clarence Gordon and spending so much time on the North Umpqua that his wife Jeanne placed an ad in the Roseburg newspaper, "Lost: One owner and manager of Moore's Cafe. Last seen up the North Umpqua River."

When Gordon offered to sell his Steamboat store to the Moores in January, 1957, Frank hastily arranged financial help from one of Gordon's regular guests, Colonel Jim Hayden, and struck a deal. That spring, the Gordons loaded all the possessions they could fit into their car and headed for a warmer climate, while the Moores took possession of the new Steamboat Inn and began constructing cabins on the bench of land just down the hill from the lodge building.

That summer of 1957 was a hectic one for the new owners. Construction continued as they wrote letters to many of the Gordons' old clients, telling them that the dam building was completed and the summer steelhead fishing had stabilized again. Each night, Jeanne Moore cooked evening meals for as many as sixty road construction crew members, who ate in shifts, before turning her attention to feeding her lodge guests. Frank pitched in, helped with the cooking, and also made a policy decision that would henceforth guide the Fisherman's Dinner: From then on, anglers could fish until the last light disappeared on the river. Dinner would be served one half hour after sunset!

In addition to his construction work at the Inn and a weekly run in his overloaded Volkswagen van to deliver food supplies to communities upstream, Moore made himself available as a fishing guide for his guests. One of the most proficient anglers on the North Umpqua, Moore's skill as a guide became one of the prime drawing cards of the Steamboat Inn in its early years.

The Steamboat Inn soon gained a reputation as both a true fisherman's resort and a family-oriented lodge. The Moore's four children mingled happily with an ever-changing cast of guests and their children. Sometimes, when the lawn was littered with the sleeping bags of children "camping out," the Inn more closely resembled summer camp than a backwoods outpost. Guests felt so much at home that they often pitched in to help serve meals from the kitchen or wash dishes afterwards.

The Fisherman's Dinner came to mirror the home-style atmosphere at the Inn. The evening meal often began with shrimp cocktail and salad, followed by soup. Entrées such as T-bone steak or prime rib roast were accompanied by vegetables, rolls, and potatoes in so much quantity "that only a logger could eat it all," as Jeanne Moore described it. Prices continued to be moderate by today's standards.

The Steamboaters

A group of Steamboat Inn regulars also evolved. They enjoyed each other's company almost as much as they enjoyed the superb angling along the North Umpqua. Colonel Jim Hayden and his wife, Laddie, were perennial guests, as were Stan Knouse, a geologist for Tidewater Oil Company in Los Angeles, and his wife, Yvonne. Ken Anderson, Art Director for Walt Disney Studios in Los Angeles, and Don Haines, a San Francisco architect, also were regular visitors. About this time, a young Salem, Oregon, lawyer named Dan Callaghan (whose scenic photos of the North Umpqua grace this cookbook) brought his bride, Mary Kay, to Steamboat for their honeymoon—beginning a long and memorable association with Cabin #1 at the Inn. Loren Grey, too, continued to make annual trips to the North Umpqua and the Steamboat Inn with his wife, Bonnie.

These anglers and their families formed the core of the group called The Steamboaters, organized in 1966. Don Haines suggested the idea for a group "to preserve the natural resources of the North Umpqua" to Colonel Jim Hayden as they traveled together to the Federation of Fly Fishers meeting in Jackson Hole, Wyoming. The Knouses and Andersons seconded the idea at a gathering the next day and Stan Knouse suggested the name Steamboaters "because of its association with the inn where many of its members stay and because of the significance of Steamboat Creek, which enters the North Umpqua at the Station Hole." Ken Anderson designed the striking logo, which is still used by the club today.

Clarence Gordon was made an honorary member of the Steamboaters, as was Roderick Haig-Brown, the eminent writer from Campbell River, British Columbia. Although he fished the river only once, Haig-Brown later wrote:

The North Umpqua remains one of the best and most beautiful of summer steelhead streams, and it has the tremendous asset of several miles of water restricted to 'fly only.' The strong flow of bright water is broken up by ledge rock outcrops,

*the pools are deep and long and hold fish well,
and the fish themselves are usually responsive
and in excellent shape.*

Unfortunately, threats to the North Umpqua's summer steelhead were again building. With the completion of a network of modern roadways into the surrounding forests, logging of the old-growth Douglas firs had begun on an unprecedented scale after World War II. Frank Moore began to notice that many of the North Umpqua's tributaries, including the crucial Steamboat Creek drainage, exhibited higher water temperatures in summer and disastrous flooding in winter, when they were scoured of spawning gravel.

In 1968, not long after the Steamboaters organization was formed, two young filmmakers, Hal Riney and Dick Snider, were on their way to make a sport-fishing movie in British Columbia when they stopped at the Steamboat Inn. They fell in love with the North Umpqua River and when Frank Moore took them on a tour of the carnage being wrought by careless logging operations in nearby tributary streams, they decided to change the focus of their film. The result was "Pass Creek," the story of the destruction of a steelhead spawning stream.

The movie was given national distribution by conservation and angling groups, touching a nerve in the emerging ecology movement. It resulted in intense scrutiny of clear-cut logging practices in the National Forests and was a factor in the passage of the Oregon Forest Practices Act. Government agencies have committed increased resources in recent years to efforts to survey and rehabilitate threatened steelhead spawning streams, including the North Umpqua drainage. Both Frank Moore and Dan Callaghan served on the Oregon State Game Commission during the 1970s and devoted tremendous energy to preserving Oregon's wildlife heritage.

Another well-known angler who frequented the North Umpqua during this period was Jack Hemingway, son of the famous author Ernest Hemingway. Himself a member of the game commission in Idaho for many years, Hemingway wrote several impassioned articles about the North Umpqua for national sporting magazines, detailing the abuses on spawning streams. Jack Hemingway, a highly skilled and graceful fly angler, continues to visit the North Umpqua to fish with his good friend, Dan Callaghan.

North Umpqua Lodge Dining Room

The Steamboat Inn Today

In 1975, Jim and Sharon Van Loan purchased the Steamboat Inn from the Moores, after working at the Inn the previous two summer seasons. Again, the ownership change signaled the end of one era—Colonel Jim Hayden had died and many other original Steamboaters were reaching the age when fishing and wading became difficult—while a new generation of anglers were stalking the banks of the North Umpqua.

Fly-fishing equipment was changing rapidly, with the old bamboo rods and silk lines giving way, first to fiberglass rods and plastic lines, then to rods made of space-age materials such as graphite and boron. All the equipment was lighter and stronger, so skilled anglers could now cast to even the most difficult holding lies of the summer steelhead. Downriver near Roseburg, a young Steamboater named Dennis Black had brought his fly-tying business from California to

Present-day Steamboat Inn Dining Room

the North Umpqua. In the next decade, his Umpqua Feather Merchants would grow from a one-man operation to become the largest wholesaler of fishing flies and fly-tying materials in the country, mirroring the skyrocketing growth of the sport of fly-fishing in the 1980s.

At the Steamboat Inn, changes were also in the works. Although Jim Van Loan worked as a textbook representative for a major publisher before purchasing the Inn, his visits to country inns in Japan during his years in military service had given him strong ideas about a new image for the Steamboat Inn. He was also careful to carry on the Inn's traditions, such as the skilled guide service he provided for guests. Along with caring for their two young children, Sarah and Jed, Sharon Van Loan taught school in those early years at the Inn. But her reputation as a chef spread so rapidly that her services at the Inn were soon required full time.

Sharon was joined by Pat Lee, who later took the title of Inn Manager. Their skills in the kitchen were particularly complementary—Pat and Sharon's sense of organization and precision blended nicely with their natural flair for matching colors and textures in food preparation. In addition, Pat Lee showed her versatility by becoming one of the most patient and respected fishing guides on the river. Tutored in the beginning by master anglers, such as Dan Callaghan, she later broke through the stereotype of the macho river guide and took her rightful place as one of the most skilled steelhead fly anglers on the North Umpqua.

In the late 1970s and early 1980s, the country inn movement was gaining strength in the United States. During this same time period, Steamboat Inn and a number of other Northwest inns established a network now known as Unique Northwest Country Inns (UNWCI). Magazine articles, guidebooks, and organizations such as UNWCI aided travelers who searched for an alternative to the plastic sameness of lodging found along the nation's interstate highways. As the Steamboat Inn appeared in guidebooks with increasing frequency, the Van Loans began to make subtle changes at the Inn to adjust to their new clientele. The riverside cabins were modernized and two more were added, bringing the total to eight. In recent years, a cluster of new cottages has been built on the bench of land above Steamboat Creek that formerly housed the Forest Service pack station in the 1930s.

The Inn itself has been extensively remodeled. A new shake roof, fresh exterior paint, and additional landscaping are the most visible changes, while the old screened rear porch has also been glassed in and weatherized, the kitchen modernized, and the family living quarters upgraded. The central dining room, with its large stone hearth and the long sugar pine dining table from the Gordon camp, has been preserved to maintain the original atmosphere.

Perhaps the most extensive changes have come in the Fisherman's Dinner itself. Still served one half hour after dark during the fishing season, the evening meal has gained elegance, while maintaining its conviviality and warmth. In keeping with modern tastes, meals are lighter, with more emphasis on fresh, native foods, prepared in a crisp style that preserves their natural flavors. Under the direction of Sharon Van Loan and Pat Lee, the Fisherman's Dinner has evolved beyond simple camp fare and become a distinctive element of the emerging Northwest cuisine.

Today's guests at the Steamboat Inn run the gamut from long-time members of Steamboat's "family" to a distinguished list of innkeepers and restaurateurs, who enjoy being pampered at the Inn while they escape the tensions of their own big-city establishments. Internationally famous anglers, such as Ernie Schwiebert, Billy Pate, Dave Whitlock, and Pierre Affre, still visit the Steamboat Inn while they search out some of the most challenging summer steelhead fly-fishing in North America.

And Jim Van Loan, following another tradition at the Inn, recently capped his many conservation activities by gaining an appointment to the Oregon Fish and Wildlife Commission.

Moreover, while today's Steamboat Inn remains firmly rooted in its fishing camp traditions, the Van Loans and Pat Lee are unafraid to experiment with new ideas or styles of food preparation. Situated far from the urban pressures of fads and trends, they are free to take what they feel is the best of the fast-changing, modern culture around them and incorporate it into their traditional setting. Best of all, they always welcome surprises.

As David Lett, the Oregon winemaker who has been called the godfather of pinot noir wines in the Willamette Valley, puts it:

Without a lot of fanfare or fussiness, Sharon and Pat create some of the most artistic and interesting food I have experienced. They incorporate an awareness of American food trends, without being 'trendy,' and would probably put a lot of 'New Wave American Cuisine' restaurants to shame.

Harry and Dolly—the originators of the Fisherman's Dinner—would be proud.

References

The authors wish to thank the following groups and individuals for their help in assembling information on the history of the Steamboat area:

The Douglas County Museum, Roseburg, Oregon.

The Umpqua National Forest, U.S. Forest Service, Roseburg, Oregon and North Umpqua Ranger District, Glide, Oregon. Special thanks to Jerry Williams.

The Steamboaters, Idleyld Park, Oregon. Special thanks to Yvonne Knouse, Memorabilia Chairperson.

Frank and Jeanne Moore, Idleyld Park, Oregon.

Loren Grey, Ph.D, Woodland Hills, California.

Merle Hargis, Idleyld Park, Oregon.

Jessie Wright, Glide, Oregon.

Recipes

Appetizers

First Course

Entrées

Rice, Potatoes, Etc.

Vegetables

Breads

Desserts

Menus and Northwest Wine Selections

Arranged in an eye-catching pattern, light and tasty hors d'oeuvres are designed to take the edge off hunger—but never compete with the carefully prepared main course.

A light soup or salad but always with a special twist, the first course offers the unexpected, challenging diners' imaginations and titillating their tastebuds.

Often arriving first is the wonderful aroma wafting out of the kitchen— perhaps with a hint of dill or a breath of chives—piquing anticipation before the bread basket is passed.

The focal point of the meal, entrées revolve around the seasons. Fresh lamb in spring, perhaps accompanied by Parmesan Potatoes, makes delicious roasts and stews.

❖

With their infinite variety of colors and interesting textures, vegetable dishes not only liven up a meal but also provide the creative cook with the chance to experiment.

◆

Many of the recipes utilized for the main course rely on the Pacific Northwest's abundant native food resources, such as fresh spring salmon, which joins a long list of available fresh fish.

Historically harvested by the early settlers in the Umpqua Valley, nuts, often combined with rice for added texture, are one of the local foods used extensively in these recipes.

The right dessert should complement the meal and provide its finishing touch, summing up the diverse elements of the various courses and leaving diners wishing for just a little more.

Appetizers

As the sun sets on another long summer day along the North Umpqua River, guests at the Steamboat Inn make their way from their cabins up the flagstone paths, through the terraced flower gardens, and arrive at the softly illuminated back porch of the Inn's main lodge.

After informal introductions, they cluster in small groups to talk about the day's events on the river. There is an easy camaraderie between gourmets and anglers, hikers and country inn fanciers. They share a love for the river and the forested mountain country all around them, a common bond that facilitates new friendships and easy conversation.

Among the anglers, there is also a shared passion for their fly-fishing quest for summer steelhead. Like fishermen everywhere, some will brag a little about their successes—and conveniently forget their defeats. They will exchange opinions on steelhead flies and favorite fishing pools, trying to learn more than they tell. Jim Van Loan mingles with dinner guests, lending an attentive ear to stories of the day's triumphs and occasionally adding a tidbit of information from his years of experience on the river. The easy camaraderie between the fishermen appeals to even the non-anglers among the guests, drawing them into the Steamboat family.

Guests will find wine and wine glasses carefully arranged in a gleaming display on the hors d'oeuvre table, their pattern quickly disrupted by eager hands. Champagne bottles, properly chilled, stand ready for the lucky fisherman with something to celebrate—or perhaps simply to commemorate another eventful day on the North Umpqua River. Carafes of crisp white wine are available, as are bottles of nonalcoholic sparkling apple cider.

Hors d'oeuvres are arranged on the polished wooden table in an eye-catching pattern. The dishes are light and tasty, designed to take the edge off hunger built up over the course of a long day on the river, but never to compete with the carefully prepared main courses yet to be served. As they talk, guests browse through the finger foods—quick bites designed for sustenance between snatches of weighty conversation.

CHÈVRE TART

This tart makes a festive addition to a holiday gathering with its red sauce, white cheese and green garnish. All of the individual components can be prepared in advance and assembled just before popping into the oven.

1 10″ or 11″ tart pan with removable bottom
1 fully baked tart shell (recipe follows)
⅓ pound Chèvre (goat cheese), in log form
1 tablespoon olive oil
¼ cup finely minced onion
2 cloves garlic, finely minced
1 28-ounce can whole tomatoes (preferably
    Italian Plum)
1½ teaspoons dried basil
½ teaspoon dried thyme
2-3 teaspoons sugar
Dash salt and pepper
1 tablespoon minced fresh parsley
    or green onion

Prepare the pastry and fully bake the tart shell according to the recipe instructions. Set aside to cool if the recipe is being prepared in advance. Using a piece of heavy thread, slice the goat cheese into ⅛″ rounds. Place on saran wrap, one layer deep. Cover and refrigerate until ready to assemble.

Heat the oil. Add the onion and garlic, and sauté until soft but not brown. Crush the tomatoes and add, along with any canned juices, to the sautéed onion and garlic. Add the basil and thyme. Simmer over medium-low heat, stirring occasionally, until thickened and reduced, about 30 minutes. (If there is too much excess liquid, it will cause the pastry to become soggy when assembled.) Add the sugar and a dash of salt and pepper. Set aside if being prepared in advance.

To assemble: Warm the sauce and spread over the cooked pastry. Cut the tart into 8 or 10 wedges and arrange one full round of goat cheese at the top of each wedge. Cut the remaining rounds in half and place one on each wedge just below the full round. If you have remaining cheese you may want to crumble and sprinkle it in the middle of the tart.

Bake in a preheated 375° oven until heated, about 8-10 minutes. Remove the tart from the oven and transfer onto a serving platter. Garnish with the parsley or green onion and serve immediately. Serves 8-10.

PLAIN FLAKY PASTRY

This is a light and flaky pastry that works well for tarts and savory turnovers.

1 cup unbleached white flour
¼ teaspoon salt
8 tablespoons chilled butter, cut into chunks
2-3 tablespoons cold water

Combine flour and salt. Cut in the butter until the mixture resembles coarse meal. Add the water one tablespoon at a time until the dough holds together. The dough may be used at this point, but it is easier to work with if it has been formed into a ball, covered with saran wrap and refrigerated for one hour. Roll out the pastry on a lightly floured board to ⅛″ thick and slightly larger in diameter than the tart pan. Place the rolled out pastry in the tart pan and press to the sides. Do not stretch the dough to make it fit. Trim excess dough by pressing your thumb along the rim of the tart pan. Chill the pastry for at least 30 minutes before baking.

Preheat the oven to 400°. Remove pastry from the refrigerator, line with foil, and weight with beans or rice (this prevents the pastry from shrinking or puffing up while baking).

For a fully baked shell: Bake 20 minutes, remove the foil and beans, and bake an additional 5 minutes until lightly browned.

For a partially baked shell: Bake 15 minutes, remove the foil and beans, and return to the oven for 2-3 minutes.

ARTICHOKE-HAM TART

This is an excellent blend of marinated artichokes, ham, and cheese in a flaky pastry. Need we say more?

1 11" tart pan with removable bottom
1 partially baked tart shell (page 43)
1 6-ounce jar marinated artichoke hearts
2 cloves garlic, minced
½ cup finely chopped onion
½ cup finely minced ham
¾ cup loosely packed grated Swiss cheese
½ cup loosely packed freshly grated
  Parmesan cheese
1 cup ricotta cheese
⅓ cup sour cream
3 eggs, lightly beaten
½ teaspoon salt
¼ teaspoon freshly ground pepper
¼ teaspoon freshly ground nutmeg

Prepare the pastry and partially bake the tart shell according to the recipe instructions. Set aside to cool.

Reserving the marinade, drain and chop the artichoke hearts. Set aside. Heat the reserved marinade in a skillet and add the garlic and onion. Cook, stirring constantly, until the vegetables are limp but not brown and the liquid in the pan has concentrated. Add the chopped hearts and sauté briefly. Set aside to cool.

Combine the ham, cheeses, sour cream, eggs, and seasonings. Add to the cooled artichoke mixture. Pour into the tart shell and bake in a preheated 375° oven 45 minutes until set. Remove from the oven and transfer to a serving platter. This tart may be served either warm or at room temperature. Serves 8-10.

SHALLOT and SUN-DRIED TOMATO TART

A nice complement to the Chèvre Tart on an hors d'oeuvre tray. The sweetness of the shallots and full flavor of the tomatoes make a wonderful combination. It seems a bit tedious to peel and mince a pound of shallots but try it! We think you will be pleased with the result!

1 11" tart pan with removable bottom
1 partially baked tart shell (page 43)
2 tablespoons olive oil
1 pound shallots, peeled and minced
2 whole green onions, minced
3-4 tablespoons minced sun-dried tomatoes
¼ teaspoon dried basil (or 2 teaspoons fresh)
2 eggs
¼ cup whipping cream
2 tablespoons minced fresh parsley
  (for garnish)

Heat the olive oil over medium heat. Add the shallots and green onion. Reduce the heat and cook until the shallots are translucent but not brown. Add the basil and sun-dried tomato. Combine well. Set aside to cool.

Beat the eggs and cream, and add the cooled shallot mixture. Pour into the partially baked tart shell and bake in a preheated 400° oven 20-25 minutes. Sprinkle with the parsley. Serves 8.

CHILLED WALNUT and CHEESE STUFFED MUSHROOMS

After the initial sampling, we were ready to discard this recipe. Instead, we refrigerated the remaining mushrooms and discovered the next day that they were very tasty—cold! This turns out to be a handy, do-ahead recipe.

4 slices thick bacon (or 5-6 thin slices, about ¼ pound)
1 pound mushrooms (about 30-40 medium)
3 tablespoons butter
½ cup minced celery
¼ cup minced whole green onion
2 tablespoons minced shallots
1 clove garlic, minced
2 ounces walnuts, toasted and chopped
2 teaspoons Worcestershire sauce
2 ounces cream cheese
5 tablespoons minced fresh parsley
3-4 tablespoons blue cheese
¾-1 teaspoon dried rosemary

Cook bacon until crisp, drain on paper towels, and finely mince. Set aside.

Wash* and stem the mushrooms. Set the caps aside and mince the stems.

Melt the butter and add the mushroom stems, celery, green onion, shallots, and garlic. Sauté 3-4 minutes until soft and most of the moisture has evaporated. Remove from the heat.

Set aside 2 tablespoons of parsley and ¼ of the minced bacon. Add the remaining bacon and parsley, walnuts, Worcestershire sauce, cream cheese, blue cheese, and rosemary to the sautéed mixture and combine well. Taste and adjust the seasonings.

Fill the caps and place on an ungreased baking sheet. Mix the reserved parsley and bacon, and garnish the tops of the mushrooms. Bake in a 400° oven 10 minutes. Remove from the oven and cool to room temperature. Chill until ready to serve. Serves 8-10.

Washing Mushrooms: Many times mushrooms need a bit more than just wiping off. Our solution has been to place the mushrooms in a plastic bag, add water and shake gently several times, changing the water if necessary. Drain the mushrooms, lay out on a kitchen towel, and pat dry.

HAM STUFFED MUSHROOMS

Another mushroom variation that is always popular with our guests. This recipe can be prepared ahead of time and heated at the last minute.

1 pound mushrooms (30-40 medium)
2 tablespoons butter
4 ounces ham, minced
2 celery stalks, minced
3 whole green onions, minced
1 large clove garlic, minced
2 tablespoons minced fresh parsley
2 teaspoons soy sauce
1 teaspoon dried tarragon
⅛ teaspoon salt
Dash cayenne
4 tablespoons freshly grated Parmesan
  cheese

Wash and stem the mushrooms. Set the caps aside and mince the stems.

Melt the butter and add the mushroom stems, ham, celery, onion, and garlic. Sauté 3-5 minutes until most of the moisture has evaporated. Remove from the heat.

Set aside 1 tablespoon of the parsley.

Add the remaining parsley, soy sauce, tarragon, salt, cayenne, and Parmesan cheese to the sautéed mixture and combine well. Taste and adjust the seasonings.

Fill the caps, rounding the tops, and place on an ungreased baking sheet. Bake in a 400° oven for 10 minutes. Arrange on a serving platter, garnish with the reserved parsley, and serve. Serves 8-10.

MUSHROOM NUT PÂTÉ

One needs to plan ahead to use this recipe, but, once finished, there are no last-minute preparations. The pâté itself doesn't lend much color to an hors d'oeuvre tray, so a second appetizer or a colorful garnish is in order.

1 whole chicken breast—cooked
6 tablespoons butter
1½ pounds mushrooms, cleaned and
  minced
1 small onion, minced (about ½ cup)
3 shallots, minced
2 cloves garlic, minced
¼ cup Madeira
1½ cup almonds, finely ground
¼ teaspoon salt
¼ teaspoon dried thyme
2 teaspoons lemon juice
Dash white pepper

Cut the chicken breast into cubes. Set aside.

Melt the butter and add the mushrooms, onion, shallots, and garlic. Cook over medium-high heat until the liquid is nearly evaporated. Add the Madeira and cook another 2-3 minutes. Remove from the heat and set aside to cool for 10 minutes.

Add the cubed chicken and the mushroom mixture to a food processor. Using several on/off turns, grind to a coarse puree. Transfer to a bowl and add the salt, thyme, lemon juice, white pepper, and ground almonds. Mix well.

Place in a mold and chill 3-4 hours. Unmold and serve with crackers or toast points. Makes 3-4 cups pâté.

SPINACH and MUSHROOM FRITTATAS

Although we normally cook this in muffin tins, when we are looking for a different shape for the hors d'oeuvre tray, we will bake this recipe in a pie plate and cut it into thin wedges. In this shape it can also be served as a first course with a light garnish of hollandaise sauce.

10 tablespoons butter
¾ pound mushrooms, cleaned and minced
5 medium shallots, minced
4 large cloves garlic, minced
20 ounces frozen spinach, thawed and
   squeezed dry
8 eggs, lightly beaten
1¼ cups freshly grated Parmesan cheese
1-1¼ teaspoons salt (amount depends on
   saltiness of the Parmesan cheese)
½ teaspoon pepper

Melt 6 tablespoons of the butter in a large skillet. Add the mushrooms, shallots, and garlic. Sauté over medium-high heat until the liquid is nearly evaporated. Reduce the heat, add the spinach, and sauté another 2 minutes, being careful not to let the spinach brown. Remove from the heat and set aside.

Combine the beaten eggs and 1 cup of the Parmesan cheese. Add the spinach mixture, salt, and pepper. Mix well.

Melt the remaining 4 tablespoons of butter and heavily coat muffin tins that have ¼ cup capacity. Fill, using 2 tablespoons of filling for each frittata. Bake 15-20 minutes in a 400° oven.* Makes 24-30 appetizers.

When using a 10" pie plate, bake 30-35 minutes in a 375° oven. Cut in large wedges. Serves 6-8 as a first course.

SEASONED LAMB and FETA in PHYLLO

A crisp and flavorful beginning to a meal—not to mention the fact that we found yet another use for ground lamb, one our guests love!

1 pound ground lamb
2 tablespoons olive oil
1 medium onion, minced (about 1 cup)
2 cloves garlic, minced
1½ teaspoons ground cumin
¾ teaspoon dried rosemary
¼ teaspoon ground allspice
½ teaspoon salt
8 ounces feta cheese, crumbled
¼ cup freshly grated Parmesan cheese
2 teaspoons lemon juice
2 eggs, lightly beaten
½ cup butter, melted
20-25 sheets phyllo dough

Brown lamb in a heavy skillet over medium heat. Remove lamb from skillet and discard all but 1 tablespoon of the pan juices. Add olive oil, onions, and garlic. Sauté until soft. Return lamb to the pan. Add cumin, rosemary, allspice, salt, cheeses, and lemon juice. Season to taste. Cool. Add beaten eggs. Makes filling for 24 rolls.

To assemble and cook: Lay out one sheet of phyllo dough, brush with melted butter, and fold lengthwise.* Place two heaping tablespoons of filling along the short edge of the dough, leaving a small margin on either side. Roll once to cover filling. Fold in the edges, brush lightly with butter, and roll up. Brush the final seam to seal it and place roll on an ungreased baking sheet. Continue with the remaining filling and phyllo. Bake 20 minutes in a 400° oven or until golden brown. Remove from the oven, cut into thirds, and serve.

Cover remaining dough with a piece of saran wrap and a towel to prevent the dough from drying out.

PETIT SHRIMP CREAM PUFFS

Our guests always enjoy the mystery of these bite-size cream puffs!

24-30 small cream puffs (see recipe for
   Jalapeño Ham Puffs page 49)
1 pound cocktail shrimp
½ cup butter
½ pound mushrooms, stemmed and sliced
   (reserve the stems for another use)
6 tablespoons minced onion
3 tablespoons minced shallots
2 cloves garlic, minced
¼ cup minced celery
½ teaspoon dry mustard
¼-½ teaspoon salt (amount depends on
   saltiness of Parmesan cheese)
Dash white pepper
¼ cup flour
2 cups half-and-half (may use part fish stock)
2 tablespoons dry sherry
1 tablespoon Dijon mustard
¼ cup freshly grated Parmesan cheese

Prepare the cream puffs per recipe instructions. When cool, slice off the tops and scoop out the interiors. Discard the interior dough and set aside the cream puffs and their tops.

Rinse the shrimp under cold water and drain on paper towels. Set aside.

Melt ¼ cup butter and add the mushrooms, onion, shallots, garlic, and celery. Sauté until soft and most of the moisture has evaporated. Set aside.

Melt the remaining ¼ cup butter. Stir in the dry mustard, salt, pepper, and flour. Cook until bubbly and thickened. Slowly stir in the half-and-half and cook, stirring constantly, until smooth and thick. Add the dry sherry and continue to cook for an additional 1-2 minutes. Remove from heat. Add the shrimp, mushroom mixture, Dijon mustard, and the Parmesan cheese. Fill the reserved cream puffs, cover the filling with the tops, and place on an ungreased baking sheet. Heat in a 350° oven for 5-10 minutes until heated through. Serves 6-8.

GINGERED SHRIMP TOASTS

This is especially well received when served on thinly sliced and toasted homemade bread. The Whole Wheat Dill, Walnut Onion or Sesame are our favorites. Just cut the thin slices into triangles, brush them with garlic butter, and toast them in a 375° oven until they are barely crisp.

½ pound cocktail shrimp
1 tablespoon sour cream
1 tablespoon cream cheese
1 teaspoon lemon juice
1 tablespoon chopped chives
2 tablespoons minced parsley
1½ tablespoons finely minced, fresh ginger
   root
Dash white pepper and cayenne
Small amount of red ginger in brine for
   garnish*

Rinse the shrimp under cool water and drain on paper towels. Divide the shrimp into two equal portions. Mince one half of the shrimp and combine it with the sour cream, cream cheese, lemon juice, chives, parsley, minced ginger, pepper, and cayenne. Fold in the reserved whole shrimp. Mix well. Refrigerate until ready to use.

Just before serving, spread the shrimp mixture on the toast triangles and garnish with strips of the red ginger. Arrange on a serving platter and garnish with fresh fruit. Serves 4-6.

This may be found in an oriental market.

JALAPEÑO HAM PUFFS

Light and spicy! Add some fresh fruit and voilà! Hors d'oeuvres!

½ cup chicken stock or water
3 tablespoons butter
½ cup flour
2 large eggs
1 medium jalapeño pepper, minced*
   (remove membrane and seeds before
   mincing)
½ cup grated Cheddar cheese, preferably
   sharp
2-3 tablespoons finely minced ham

Place water and butter in a saucepan over medium heat. Cook until the butter is melted. Add the flour all at once and stir well to combine. Cook until the mixture holds together and pulls away from the sides of the pan, stirring constantly. Remove from the heat and cool briefly.

Add the eggs, one at a time, beating well after each addition. Fold in the remaining ingredients.

Place small, walnut-sized mounds 2" apart on an ungreased cookie sheet that has been sprinkled with water. Bake in a preheated 400° oven 15-20 minutes. Makes 20-24 small puffs.

When working with the hot peppers, be sure to wear plastic gloves and keep your hands away from your eyes and face.

To use as regular cream puffs: Increase the butter to ¼ cup, add ⅛ teaspoon salt, and omit the peppers, cheese, and ham. Prepare and bake as stated above.

JALAPEÑO and DRY JACK WONTONS

These tasty wontons take a minimum amount of preparation time and are guaranteed to get rave reviews, especially when served with your favorite guacamole.

30 wonton wrappers*
¼ pound dry Monterey Jack cheese, grated
2 medium jalapeño peppers, minced**
   (remove membrane and seeds before
   mincing)
2 small whole green onions, minced
Oil for deep frying

Combine the cheese, peppers, and onions. Place 1 heaping teaspoon of filling in the middle of a wonton. Brush the edges with water, fold into a triangle and press the edges to seal. Set aside on a rack and continue with the remaining filling and wontons.

Using a heavy-bottomed saucepan, place 2" of oil in the bottom and heat to 350°. Place a few wontons at a time in the hot oil and cook on both sides until crisp and brown. Remove and drain on paper towels. Continue with the remaining wontons and serve while still warm. Serves 6.

Wonton wrappers can usually be found in the produce section of your grocery store. They freeze well so it is easy to keep them on hand.

**When working with the hot peppers, be sure to wear plastic gloves and keep your hands away from your eyes and face.*

CURRIED PORK TURNOVERS

Even though these start with "left-over" pork, it is a sure bet there will not be any leftover turnovers! Crisp, juicy apples are an excellent complement to the curry and pork in these tasty morsels.

1 recipe Plain Flaky Pastry (page 43)
½ pound cooked pork, ground
3 tablespoons olive oil
½ cup minced onion
3 cloves garlic, minced
2 stalks celery, minced
¼ pound mushrooms, cleaned and minced
2 teaspoons minced fresh ginger root
1 medium tomato, seeded and finely cubed
½ teaspoon turmeric
½ teaspoon salt
1 teaspoon cumin
¼ teaspoon white pepper
¼ cup minced fresh parsley
2 tablespoons plain yogurt
1 egg, beaten with 1 tablespoon water (for egg wash)

Heat the olive oil in a skillet and add the onions and garlic. Sauté 3-4 minutes until they start to soften. Add the celery, mushrooms, and ginger. Continue to cook until most of the liquid has evaporated and the vegetables are soft but not brown. Remove from the heat and add the pork, tomato, turmeric, salt, cumin, white pepper, parsley, and yogurt. Mix well. Set aside to cool.

Roll out the pastry and cut into 3-4" rounds. Place 2-3 teaspoons of filling in the center of the round. Brush the edges with the egg wash, fold over, and seal. Place on an ungreased baking sheet. Continue with the remaining filling and pastry. Brush the tops of the turnovers with the remaining egg wash and bake in a 375-400° oven 20-25 minutes. Makes about 36 turnovers. If you have more filling than you need, it freezes well.

CHERRY TOMATOES and SNOW PEAS with SEASONED CHEESE

The cherry tomatoes and snow peas add a splash of color to any hors d'oeuvre tray.

1 dozen medium-size cherry tomatoes
1 dozen snow peas
4 ounces cream cheese
¼-½ teaspoon finely minced garlic
1 tablespoon finely minced chives
2 teaspoons finely minced fresh parsley
2 tablespoons finely minced fresh spinach
½ teaspoon Worcestershire sauce
2 tablespoons finely minced ham or shrimp (optional)

Wash the tomatoes. Cut a thin slice off the top and seed. Place upside down on a rack to drain.

Remove the stem from the snow peas, string them, and blanch in a pot of boiling water for 30 seconds. Remove from the heat and immediately plunge into ice water to stop the cooking process. Lay out on paper towels to drain. With a sharp knife carefully open up the pods along their straight side.

Combine the cream cheese, garlic, chives, parsley, spinach, Worcestershire sauce, and minced ham or shrimp. Mix well. Taste and adjust, keeping in mind the fact that the longer this sets the stronger the flavors will be.

Using a pastry bag fitted with an open tip, pipe about 2 teaspoons of filling into each of the cherry tomatoes and snow peas. Makes 24 appetizers.

SPICY CHICKEN WINGS

When finger foods are the order of the day, this is always a big winner with just the right amount of spice! The ingredients are inexpensive and easy to keep on hand. A garnish of crisp red apple and a bit of parsley add a nice finish to the platter.

10 whole chicken wings (about 1¾ pounds)
¼ cup plus 1 tablespoon water
2 tablespoons light soy sauce
2 tablespoons honey
2 tablespoons hot sauce (we use Pico Pica®)
1 teaspoon tomato paste
2 teaspoons cornstarch
1 tablespoon vegetable oil
2 teaspoons finely minced fresh ginger root
1 tablespoon minced fresh garlic
3 tablespoons cornstarch, for dusting
    the wings
Oil for deep frying

Cut the wings into three sections, reserving the small tips for another use. Set the two larger sections aside.

Combine the water, soy sauce, honey, hot sauce, and tomato paste. Mix well. Blend in the 2 teaspoons cornstarch and set aside.

Heat the 1 tablespoon of oil in a small, heavy-bottomed pan over high heat until hot. Add the ginger and garlic, and immediately reduce the heat so they sizzle but do not brown. Stir for less than one minute, then add the reserved liquid mixture. Let the pan ingredients come to a simmer. Continue to cook and stir until thickened and glossy. Set aside.

Using a heavy-bottomed saucepan, place 2" of oil in the bottom and heat to 350°.

While the oil is heating, lightly dust the wing pieces with the remaining 3 tablespoons of cornstarch.

Deep fry the wings in small batches until golden brown. (Be careful—overcooking will dry them out.) Drain on several layers of paper towels. (They may be held in a low oven up to 30 minutes at this point.)

Just before serving, reheat the sauce and toss with the wings until they are well coated. Serve hot. Makes 20 pieces or serves 4-6.

HERBED CHICKEN STRIPS

This is another recipe where the individual components can be assembled far in advance, then combined and finished off in a matter of minutes. The resulting appetizer is crisp and flavorful on the outside and tender and juicy on the inside.

1 whole chicken breast, boned and cut into
    ¼" × 1" strips (about 10 ounces after
    boning)
¼ cup flour
½ teaspoon onion salt
½ teaspoon paprika
⅛ teaspoon dried sage
⅛ teaspoon dried oregano
1 egg, lightly beaten
¼ cup chicken stock or water
¼ cup loosely packed, freshly grated
    Parmesan cheese
oil for deep frying

Combine the flour, onion salt, paprika, sage, and oregano. Mix well. Combine the egg, chicken stock, and Parmesan cheese, and add to the dry ingredients. Mix well.

Using a heavy-bottomed saucepan, place 2" of oil in the bottom and heat to 350°. Dip the chicken pieces in the batter and fry in the hot oil until golden brown—about 3 minutes. Drain on paper towels, arrange on a serving platter, and serve hot. Serves 4-6.

SESAME CHEESE WAFERS

These wafers will have several uses when you are planning for appetizers. They are a flavorful, crisp addition to most light soups or an excellent contrast in texture to a soft appetizer such as stuffed mushrooms. You will see them disappear first if you include them in an assortment of crackers for spreads or pâtés.

6 ounces cheese, grated (about 1½ cups*)
½ cup freshly grated Parmesan cheese
¾ cup white flour
¼ cup wheat germ
¼ cup sesame seeds
¼ teaspoon dry mustard
¼ cup butter
1 tablespoon (or more) cold water
1 teaspoon Worcestershire sauce

Combine the cheeses, flour, wheat germ, sesame seeds, and mustard. Cut in the butter. Mix one tablespoon of water with the Worcestershire sauce and add to the dough. (The dough may need a few more drops of water to bind it.) Form into a log 1½" in diameter, wrap in saran, and refrigerate until firm.

Cut into ⅛" wafers and place on an ungreased baking sheet. Bake in a 400° oven 20-30 minutes. Makes 24-30 wafers.

We often use ½ Cheddar and ½ jalapeño jack cheese.

First Course

When evening falls, the Steamboat Inn is transformed. The blinds are drawn and the "Closed for the Evening" sign is hung in the window. Inside, the setting is dramatic but comfortably intimate. Overhead lights are dimmed and replaced with the soft glow from oil lamps and candles. Classical music—tonight it's Vivaldi's *Four Seasons*—filters into the dining room through the sound system. In the oversized stone fireplace, a fire burns briskly. The long, massive sugar pine table is bedecked with freshly picked flowers, white tablecloths, china, shining silver, and wine glasses that reflect the candlelight. The prelude is over, and dinner is about to begin.

In the kitchen, Pat Lee and Sharon Van Loan supervise the cooking crew in the final stages of preparing the evening meal. There are a hundred details to attend to (at least!) and never enough time. But somehow, thanks to the skills acquired over years of working together, Sharon and Pat mysteriously manage to whisk each course together in time. A final check of the first course, with a critical eye for color and design, and it's time to put out the call: Dinner is served in the main dining room.

Guests arrange themselves on either side of the long table, finding their places on the shiny pine benches that run its full length. Discussions begun during hors d'oeuvres may continue, or perhaps another round of introductions is in order to initiate conversation with new dinner companions. Both red and white wines are on the table, decanted into carafes and ready to be poured. More adventuresome diners may choose a bottle of wine from the Steamboat Inn's small but distinctive list of Oregon varietal wines. Anticipation is in the air, as though the curtain were about to go up on an exciting first act.

The first course has already been placed in front of each guest. It's often a light soup or salad but always with a special twist. Pat and Sharon delight in experimenting with new combinations of texture and color in the first course. Would almonds and carrots make an interesting pair? Or perhaps leeks with ham and cranberries? The guests are never quite sure what to expect—only that their imaginations will be challenged and their tastebuds titillated.

So without any further ado, it's time to begin the Fisherman's Dinner at the Steamboat Inn.

HERBED WALNUT SALAD

This often-requested salad lends itself to a multitude of variation and is an interesting use of walnuts. Try substituting Raspberry Vinegar (page 56) for the white wine vinegar and adding fresh watercress and thinly sliced red onion. The Walnut Vinaigrette offers a nice finish to almost any salad.

2 small heads butter lettuce or 1 larger head
   red or green leaf
¼ cup freshly grated Parmesan cheese
½ cup walnuts, coarsely chopped
1 tablespoon walnut oil
¼ teaspoon dried basil
¼ teaspoon dried rosemary
Walnut Vinaigrette (recipe follows)

Wash the lettuce and refrigerate until ready to use. Heat the walnut oil over low heat. Add the walnuts, basil, and rosemary. Sauté, stirring constantly, until the nuts are lightly toasted. Be careful! The nut and herb combination burns easily. Set aside to cool.

Tear the washed lettuce into a serving bowl. Add ¾ of the seasoned walnuts, all of the Parmesan cheese, and half of the vinaigrette. Toss to coat the greens, adding more vinaigrette as necessary. Arrange on plates and garnish with the reserved walnuts. Serves 6-8.

WALNUT VINAIGRETTE

¼ cup vegetable oil
2 tablespoons walnut oil
3 tablespoons white wine vinegar
3 cloves garlic, minced
½ teaspoon salt
¼ teaspoon pepper

Combine the oils, vinegar, garlic, salt, and pepper. Mix well.

FRESH TOMATO and SPINACH SALAD with BASIL VINAIGRETTE

A refreshing summer salad! We only serve this when tomatoes are in season locally, as hothouse tomatoes do not have the same effect.

6 cups thinly sliced spinach
3-4 large, ripe, full-flavored tomatoes, cut in
   ¼" slices
⅓ cup vegetable oil
2 tablespoons red, white or Raspberry
   Vinegar (page 56)
1 clove garlic, finely minced
⅓ cup freshly grated Parmesan cheese,
   tightly packed (about 1 ounce)
2 tablespoons finely minced parsley
1 tablespoon fresh basil leaves, minced
   (or 1 teaspoon dried)
1 teaspoon sugar
1 teaspoon salt
Dash freshly ground pepper

Combine the oil, vinegar, garlic, Parmesan cheese, parsley, basil, sugar, salt, and pepper. Mix well.

Divide the spinach among 6 salad plates. Arrange 3 tomato slices on top of each plate of spinach. Drizzle the vinaigrette over the top of the tomatoes and serve. Serves 6.

SPINACH SALAD

As pleasing to the eye as it is to the palate, this salad brings quizzical looks, as your guests try to place the flavorful blend of the fresh pear, blue cheese, and Raspberry Vinegar.

1 large bunch fresh spinach
⅓ cup sliced almonds, toasted
2 tablespoons crumbled blue cheese
1 whole green onion, thinly sliced
1 Red Delicious apple
1 small, ripe pear
6 tablespoons vegetable oil
3 tablespoons Raspberry Vinegar (recipe
    follows)
⅛ teaspoon salt
Dash freshly grated nutmeg

Wash the spinach and refrigerate until ready to use. Peel, core, and halve the pear. Place one pear half in a blender along with the oil, vinegar, salt, and nutmeg. Puree and set aside.

Thinly slice the remaining pear half and place in lemon water to prevent discoloration. Drain before using. Core the apple and cut into fourths. Cut ¾ of the apple into chunks and thinly slice the remaining ¼.

Tear the washed spinach into a serving bowl. Add the almonds, blue cheese, thinly sliced green onion, and the apple chunks. Add half of the dressing. Toss to coat the greens, adding more dressing as necessary. Arrange on serving plates and garnish the tops with the apple and pear slices. Serves 6.

◆

RASPBERRY VINEGAR

2 cups white wine vinegar
3 tablespoons sugar (more if your berries are
    especially tart)
¾ cup raspberries, fresh or frozen

Bring the vinegar to a boil and add the sugar. Reduce the heat and stir until the sugar is dissolved. Simmer 5 minutes.

Place the berries in a glass jar and add the hot vinegar. When cool, cover with cheesecloth and let stand 48 hours to season. Strain, bottle, and store in a cool place. Use whenever a sweet-sour taste is desired.

FIRST COURSE

SPINACH, BACON, and JICAMA SALAD

A crunchy, colorful, and satisfying salad. The ingredients, simple and easy to prepare, create a finished salad that will complement any menu.

1 large bunch fresh spinach
2 tablespoons vegetable oil
2 tablespoons olive oil
3 tablespoons white wine vinegar
1 teaspoon sugar
½ teaspoon Dijon mustard
⅛ teaspoon salt
Dash freshly ground pepper
6 ounces (4-5 slices) thick bacon
6 ounces jicama, cut in 1" long julienne
2 ounces Swiss cheese, grated
1 cup thinly sliced red cabbage

Wash the spinach and refrigerate until ready to use.

Combine the vegetable oil, olive oil, vinegar, sugar, mustard, salt, and freshly ground pepper. Mix well. Chill until ready to use.

Slice the bacon into ¼-inch pieces and cook until crisp but not overly brown. Drain on paper towels and set aside.

Tear the washed spinach into a serving bowl. Add the bacon, jicama, Swiss cheese, and red cabbage. Toss to combine. Stir the dressing and toss with the salad. Mix well. Arrange on serving plates and serve immediately. Serves 6-8.

TORTELLINI and MIXED GREENS

A hearty salad often used to round out a menu that feels a bit light, or it may also be used as a main luncheon course.

½ cup vegetable oil
2 tablespoons olive oil
2 tablespoons white wine vinegar
2 tablespoons balsamic vinegar
2 cloves garlic, finely minced
⅓ cup freshly grated Parmesan cheese, tightly packed (about 1 ounce)
1 teaspoon dried basil
1 teaspoon sugar
¼ teaspoon salt
⅛ teaspoon freshly ground pepper
1 tablespoon minced fresh parsley
1 9-ounce package fresh tortellini*
12 cups mixed greens (spinach, romaine, red and green leaf lettuce)

Combine the oils, vinegars, garlic, Parmesan cheese, basil, sugar, salt, and pepper. Mix well.

Cook the tortellini per package instructions. Drain, place in a bowl, and toss with the minced parsley and ¼-½ cup dressing. Set aside to cool.

Toss the greens with some of the dressing until coated and arrange on 6 serving plates. Top with the tortellini and serve. Serves 6 as a first course or 4 as a main luncheon course.

*Fresh tortellini can usually be found in the cheese or produce department of your grocery store.

CARROT ALMOND SALAD

We serve this as a colorful topping to fresh greens or as an addition to a brunch or antipasto plate (with extra for the kitchen crew, of course!).

1 pound carrots, cleaned and *coarsely* grated
⅔ cup sliced almonds, lightly toasted
¼ cup Soy Dressing (recipe follows)

Combine the grated carrots and almonds. Add ¼ cup Soy Dressing and mix well. Serves 4-6 on an antipasto plate. Serves 8 when used as a topping for fresh greens.

SOY DRESSING

⅓ cup rice wine vinegar
⅓ cup vegetable oil
3 tablespoons soy sauce
1 large clove garlic, minced
2 teaspoons minced fresh ginger root

Combine the above ingredients and mix well. Makes about ¾ cup dressing.

CARROT TART

A good friend introduced Steamboat Inn to the idea of carrots being used in a tart a number of years ago. Our flaky pastry and added seasonings have produced a simple, do-ahead recipe—one that is an often-requested hit.

1 10″-11″ tart pan with removable bottom
1 fully baked tart shell (page 43)
1½ pounds carrots, peeled and cut in
   ¼″ slices
1 teaspoon sugar
2 tablespoons butter, room temperature
1 teaspoon lemon juice
¼ teaspoon dill weed
¼ teaspoon salt
2 dashes cayenne pepper
1 tablespoon chopped fresh chives or
   minced parsley, for garnish

Place the sliced carrots and sugar in a pot of boiling salted water. Cook 10-12 minutes until the carrots are tender but crisp. Drain. For garnish, select and set aside 8 slices each of small, medium, and large diameter slices.

Transfer the remaining carrots to the work bowl of a food processor and process until the carrots are a coarse puree. Add the butter, lemon juice, dill weed, salt, and cayenne. Combine with 2 pulses of the processor.

Transfer the mixture to the fully baked tart shell and spread in an even layer over the bottom of the shell. Cut the tart into 8 wedges. Garnish each wedge with 3 of the reserved carrot slices—starting with the largest at the outer edge, following with the medium, and ending up with the smallest slice at the apex of the wedge.

Bake in a preheated 400° oven for about 10 minutes, until heated through. Sprinkle with the chives or parsley and transfer to individual serving plates. Serve immediately. Serves 8.

NAPA CABBAGE and FILBERT SALAD

This salad evolved one year when buying salad greens was comparable to buying gold! It was so well received that it has become one of our favorites. We frequently use it during the holidays, when its intense red garnish is especially appealing.

1 cup whole filberts, toasted, the skins rubbed off and then split in half
4 cups thinly sliced napa cabbage
1 small raw beet, *coarsely* grated
4 ounces (¼ pound) thinly sliced ham, cut in julienne
6 tablespoons white wine vinegar
3 tablespoons filbert oil*
3 tablespoons vegetable oil
1 tablespoon minced whole green onion
2 tablespoons minced fresh parsley
1 large or 2 small cloves garlic, minced
2 teaspoons Dijon mustard
½ teaspoon salt
½ teaspoon sugar
1 bunch watercress (for garnish)

Combine the vinegar, oils, green onion, parsley, garlic, mustard, salt, and sugar. Mix well. Toss the grated beet with 2 tablespoons of the dressing. In a separate bowl, toss the ham with 2 tablespoons of the dressing. Add the filberts and thinly sliced napa cabbage to the ham. Mix well. Add ¼ cup of the dressing and toss to coat, adding more dressing as necessary. Arrange the watercress around the rim of 4 salad plates. Place ¼ of the salad in the middle of each of the plates and top with the grated beets. Serves 4.

Filbert oil, labeled as hazelnut oil, may be found on the specialty aisle of your grocery store.

RED CABBAGE with WALNUTS and BLUE CHEESE

This salad variation takes advantage of our Walnut Vinaigrette and the great blue cheese from the Rogue Valley Creamery.

¾ pound red cabbage, thinly sliced
1-2 tablespoons blue cheese, crumbled
3 tablespoons toasted walnuts, coarsely chopped
6 tablespoons Walnut Vinaigrette (page 55)

Toss all of the ingredients, mixing well. Serve on an antipasto plate or as a topping for fresh greens. Serves 4-6.

SESAME ASPARAGUS

A colorful and tasty addition to an antipasto plate. Snow peas are an acceptable substitute when fresh asparagus is unavailable.

1 pound asparagus
3 tablespoons vegetable oil
3 tablespoons sesame oil
3 tablespoons white wine vinegar
3 tablespoons soy sauce
1 large clove garlic, minced
2 teaspoons minced fresh ginger root
¼ cup toasted sesame seeds

Lightly blanch the asparagus (or snow peas) in boiling water, leaving the vegetables very crisp. Drain and immerse in ice water to stop the cooking process. Chill until ready to use.

Combine the oils, vinegar, soy sauce, garlic, and ginger. Mix well. Just before serving, toss the asparagus with enough dressing to coat and flavor it. Garnish with the sesame seeds. Serves 4-6.

LEEK SALAD with HAM and CRANBERRIES

A couple of years ago a local organic gardener (who was also our flower gardener) supplied us with an overabundance of leeks, and the following recipe is the result of one of our many experiments.

12 small leeks
6 cups chicken stock
½ cup cranberries
2 ounces ham, chopped
1 tablespoon minced fresh parsley
¼ cup olive oil
2 tablespoons vegetable oil
2 tablespoons lemon juice
1 teaspoon Dijon mustard
2 garlic cloves, minced
½-1 teaspoon salt (start with the smaller amount and add more as necessary)
Freshly ground pepper

Wash and trim the leeks, using all the white portion and 4" of the green. Set aside. Bring the chicken stock to a boil and add the cranberries. Cook the berries *just until* they begin to pop. Remove with a slotted spoon and set aside.

Tie the leeks together in bunches of three and add to the stock. Reduce the heat to a simmer and cook 10 minutes until softened. Remove from the stock and cool. Set the stock aside for another use. (It will be a little cloudy but will have a wonderful flavor.)

Combine the parsley, the oils, lemon juice, Dijon mustard, garlic, salt, and pepper. Mix well. Combine the ham and cranberries and add 2 tablespoons of the dressing. Arrange 3 leeks on each of four salad plates and drizzle with a small amount of the dressing. Top with the ham/cranberry mixture. Serves 4.

WARM CHICKEN LIVER and JULIENNE VEGETABLE SALAD

This recipe requires advanced planning but the extra preparation time is worth the effort! Make sure all the individual components are prepped before you begin the final assembly. This should be served immediately to receive the full effect of the seasonings, crisp vegetables, and warm chicken livers.

2 cups, thinly sliced, fresh spinach
5 ounces chicken livers (filament and fat removed)
4 ounces carrots, cut in 1" julienne
4 ounces zucchini, cut in 1" julienne (use only the firm outer layer)
3 ounces snow peas, julienne (using a diagonal cut)
4 tablespoons butter
2 tablespoons minced shallots
3 ounces stemmed mushrooms, sliced
1 whole green onion, minced
¼ cup chicken stock
3 tablespoons Raspberry Vinegar (page 56)
1 teaspoon Dijon mustard
1 teaspoon dried tarragon
Dash salt, pepper, and cayenne

Divide the spinach among 4 serving plates. Cut each of the chicken livers into 4 pieces. Blanch the carrots, zucchini, and snow peas—one vegetable at a time—in lightly salted water until tender but crisp. Drain and immerse in ice water to stop the cooking process. Drain and lay on a towel. Melt the butter and sauté the shallots until they start to soften. Add the mushrooms and the chicken livers. Cook, stirring constantly, until the livers are heated through and lightly pink inside. Toss in the minced green onion and stir to combine. Using a slotted spoon, transfer the chicken liver mixture to a heated platter.

Deglaze the pan with the chicken stock and Raspberry Vinegar. Add the mustard, tarragon, salt, pepper, and cayenne. Cook until the mixture begins to thicken. Spoon 2 tablespoons of the pan juices over the chicken livers. Add the blanched vegetables to the remaining liquid in the pan and stir over medium heat just long enough to heat the vegetables.

Using a slotted spoon, transfer the vegetables to the individual serving plates, arranging them on top of the spinach. Return the chicken livers and any accumulated juices to the pan and stir until just heated through. Immediately arrange on top of the vegetables and serve. Serves 4.

BROCCOLI and FLANK STEAK SALAD

This salad makes a hearty first course. It stands alone as a main luncheon course when served on a bed of fresh spinach or romaine. With the addition of a roll or slice of bread, you have a complete meal, offering a variety of texture and color.

1 pound broccoli, cut into spears and peeled (reserve stem ends for another use)
8 ounces (½ pound) cooked flank steak or beef tenderloin
1 cup thinly sliced red cabbage
½-¾ cup Soy Dressing (page 58)
2 tablespoons toasted sesame seeds (optional)

Lightly blanch the broccoli in salted water. Drain and immerse in ice water to stop the cooking process. (The broccoli should be very green and crisp.) Drain, lay out on a towel, and set aside. Slice the cooked meat across the grain into ¼" strips and cut the strips into 1½" pieces. Toss with some of the dressing and set aside. In another bowl, toss the sliced cabbage with some of the dressing. Arrange the broccoli, marinated flank steak, and marinated cabbage in an interesting pattern on serving plates. Garnish with toasted sesame seeds if desired. Makes 3-4 luncheon or 8 first course servings.

CURRIED ZUCCHINI SOUP

When a creamed soup is not a cream soup! We prefer most of our "creamed" soups with a clear, uncomplicated flavor which occurs with a combination of a good stock, a hint of onion and/or garlic, the base flavor (in this case, zucchini), and a light herb accent. With well-balanced flavors, it is a shame to dilute the soup with an addition of cream.

4 tablespoons butter
3 small shallots, minced
2 cloves garlic, minced
1½ pounds zucchini, thinly sliced
2 cups chicken stock
¼ cup dry white wine
2 tablespoons freshly grated Parmesan cheese
1½ teaspoons curry
¼ teaspoon cumin
¼ teaspoon salt (omit if using canned stock)
Dash cayenne

Melt the butter over medium heat. Add the shallots and garlic. Cook 2 minutes, stirring constantly. Add the sliced zucchini, wine, and ½ cup stock. Cover, reduce the heat, and simmer 10 minutes, until the zucchini is tender. Cool, transfer to a blender, and puree. Return to a 2-quart saucepan and add the remaining stock, Parmesan cheese, curry, cumin, salt (if necessary), and cayenne. Heat and simmer 3-4 minutes to let the flavors meld. Taste and adjust as necessary. Serves 4.

BAKED EGGPLANT with CURRIED TOMATO SAUCE

Over the years we have "won-over" many non-eggplant eaters with this recipe. It evolved from a festive evening of Afghan food prepared by a guest chef. We loved the flavors but found the food heavy with oil. We feel we have saved all the tantalizing flavors while eliminating the oily aftertaste.

1 large onion, minced
6 cloves garlic, minced
½ cup plus 1 tablespoon olive oil
1¾ cup chicken stock
6 ounces tomato paste
¼ teaspoon chili powder
½ teaspoon salt
1 teaspoon curry powder
1 teaspoon ground cumin
Freshly ground pepper
¾ cup plain yogurt or sour cream
½ teaspoon garlic powder
½ teaspoon garlic salt
24 ⅜" slices, peeled eggplant (about
    3 pounds)
Coarse (sea) salt
½ cup minced fresh parsley

Sauté the onion and half of the garlic in 1 tablespoon of olive oil until soft but not brown. Add the stock, tomato paste, chili powder, salt, curry, cumin, and freshly ground pepper. Simmer 1 hour until thickened. (This may be done ahead and reheated prior to serving.) Combine the yogurt, garlic powder, and garlic salt. Mix well. Set aside.

Sprinkle the eggplant rounds with the coarse salt and lay out on towels. After 30 minutes wipe off the salt and any accumulated moisture. Use an absorbent towel. If not done thoroughly you will have salty eggplant!

Combine the remaining olive oil and garlic, and brush both sides of the eggplant slices. Place on a baking sheet and bake 30 minutes in a preheated 350° oven.*

Depending on the size of the eggplant slices, use two or three per plate, overlapping them slightly. Top each slice with 1 heaping tablespoon of spicy red sauce, then 2 teaspoons seasoned yogurt, and a sprinkling of parsley. Serves 8-12 as a first course.

Be prepared to assemble the plates as soon as the eggplant is removed from the oven.

BROCCOLI TIMBALES

A rich first course that we have presented with a Curry Bacon Sauce.

6 individual molds, ¾ cup capacity, buttered
1 tablespoon butter
2 tablespoons minced shallots
1 clove garlic, minced
½ cup whipping cream
1 cup rich chicken stock (preferably homemade)
4 eggs, beaten
½ cup freshly grated Parmesan cheese
½ teaspoon salt
Dash freshly grated nutmeg
Dash black pepper
1½ cups finely chopped cooked broccoli
Dash lemon juice
Curry Bacon Sauce (recipe follows)

Melt the butter and briefly sauté the shallots and garlic. Set aside.

Combine the cream, stock, beaten eggs, Parmesan cheese, salt, nutmeg, pepper, and lemon juice to taste. Add the broccoli, sautéed shallots, and garlic to the cream mixture. Pour into 6 individual buttered molds, and place the molds in a baking pan. Fill the pan with hot water to the level of the filling in the molds.

Bake in a preheated 325° oven until a knife inserted in the center of a timbale comes out clean, about 20-30 minutes. Invert onto a serving plate and cover with Curry Bacon Sauce. Serves 4 as a first or luncheon course.

CURRY BACON SAUCE

1 teaspoon unsalted butter*
2 tablespoons minced whole green onions
½ teaspoon curry powder
Pinch of dried thyme
¼ cup chicken stock
½ cup whipping cream
1 slice thick bacon, cooked crisp and minced

Melt the butter in a small saucepan over medium heat. Add the green onions and sauté until they are soft. Reduce heat and add the curry and thyme. Cook, stirring constantly, for 5 minutes. Add the stock and cream. Continue to cook until reduced and slightly thickened. Remove from the heat and add the minced bacon. Serve warm over the broccoli timbales.

*If you are using canned stock the unsalted butter is important. Otherwise, you will end up with a salty sauce.

Entrées

Long, strenuous days on the river make for hearty appetites. The main courses of the Fisherman's Dinner—the entrées, vegetables, and potatoes, rice or pasta—are consumed in prodigious amounts by hungry guests. Many of the recipes utilized for the main courses rely on the abundant native food resources of the Pacific Northwest. Sharon and Pat stress preparation techniques that preserve the clean, natural flavors of the foods.

Entrées revolve around the seasons. Fresh lamb in spring makes delicious roasts and stews. As the salmon return to the rivers, they join the long list of fresh fish available to the eager chefs in the Steamboat Inn kitchen. Summer's heat drives the cooks from the kitchen and encourages them to use the barbecue in the evening—for mouth-watering salmon fillets, lamb chops, and beef tenderloins.

Many of the traditional, heavy entrées from the old fishing camps along the river have been replaced in Pat and Sharon's Fisherman's Dinner by lighter dishes. Chicken Breasts with Orange Thyme Butter Sauce combines surprising flavors in an entrée that's easy on calories, as well as on the palate. Scallops in Feta Cream Sauce utilizes a resource from the ocean waters off Oregon in a satisfying, new way. And Red Snapper with Jalapeño Lime Marinade guarantees to spice up any evening.

Conversation levels are subdued among the guests, now that the main courses are center stage. It takes extreme concentration to derive full enjoyment from such delicious fare! But even good food can't keep a group as diverse as this quiet, for a spicy entrée jars loose memories of a day's fishing for big rainbow trout in some icy Chilean lake.

The wine flows and the main dishes are passed around the table one more time. The names of bright trout rivers mingle lightly with Mozart and the cool evening air. After a day spent next to deep river pools, an evening of sharp river memories, soul-satisfying repast, and intriguing new friends emerges.

CHICKEN BREAST with ORANGE THYME BUTTER SAUCE

A rich centerpiece for a winter dinner party. This recipe needs only the simplest accompaniment—a bit of Orzo*, steamed broccoli, and a citrus dessert.

5 whole chicken breasts, skinned, boned, and cut in half
2 cups undiluted orange juice concentrate
1¼ cups chilled butter
¾ cup flour
1 tablespoon plus 2 teaspoons fresh thyme leaves
Dash salt and pepper
¾ cup dry white wine
3 tablespoons minced shallots
2 tablespoons minced Candied Orange Slices (page 115)
1 tablespoon whipping cream

Soak the chicken breasts in the orange juice concentrate for 4 hours.

Combine the flour, 1 tablespoon thyme, salt, and pepper. Remove the breasts from the concentrate and dredge in the flour mixture. Shake off any excess. Melt 2 tablespoons of the butter in a skillet over medium heat and sauté half of the breasts 1-2 minutes per side, until lightly browned. Place the breasts on a baking sheet and continue with 2 more tablespoons butter and the remaining breasts. Bake in a preheated 350° oven until heated through and the juices run clear when the breasts are pierced with a fork, about 10 minutes.

While the breasts are in the oven, combine the white wine, shallots, candied orange slices, and remaining thyme in a non-corrosive pan. Reduce over medium heat, until 2-3 tablespoons of liquid remain. Reduce the heat to low and begin whisk-ing in the remaining 1 cup butter—2 tablespoons at a time—until it has all been incorporated. Stir in the whipping cream to bind the sauce. Top each breast with 1 tablespoon of the butter sauce. Serves 6-8.

*Orzo, a rice-shaped pasta, will yield 4 servings per cup. Add it to a pot of rapidly boiling water and cook 20 minutes until doubled in size. It finishes off quickly with salt, pepper, freshly grated Parmesan, and minced parsley; otherwise, it may be tossed with a sauce you may be using elsewhere in your menu.

BARBECUED BONELESS CHICKEN BREASTS

A quick, light, and flavorful entrée. An excellent choice for a warm summer evening.

5 whole chicken breasts, skinned, boned, and cut in half
¼ cup honey
¼ cup vegetable oil
¼ cup soy sauce
¼ cup Yukon Jack*
3 large garlic cloves, minced
4 whole green onions, minced
¼ teaspoon salt
Dash cayenne
1 large lemon, cut in 6 pieces

Combine the honey, oil, soy sauce, and Yukon Jack. Mix well. Add the garlic, green onions, salt, and cayenne. Squeeze each of the lemon pieces over the mixture and then drop the piece into the marinade. Add the chicken breasts, toss to coat, and let marinate 4 hours.

Barbecue over a medium-hot fire 3-4 minutes per side, basting as they cook. Serves 6-8.

*You may use bourbon or scotch as a substitute.

CHICKEN ROLL with SCALLOPS and SHRIMP

With this recipe you will need to plan ahead in your preparations, allowing ample time for the final assembly.

1 3½-pound chicken, boned with skin intact*
2 large shallots
3 ounces chicken fat
8 ounces raw shrimp, peeled and deveined
2 teaspoons lemon juice
¼ teaspoon salt
Dash white pepper
1 teaspoon minced fresh thyme
⅓ cup scallop juice or chicken stock
⅓ cup whipping cream
3 tablespoons butter
1 large garlic clove, minced
6 ounces bay scallops

Place the boned chicken skin side down on a work surface. You will notice there are a couple of places where there is no meat on the skin. Cover these areas with the two loose breast fillets. Cover the meat with saran. Using the flat side of a large cleaver pound the chicken to flatten it. Trim ½″ off the lower edge of each leg area and any excess skin. You should end up with a rectangular-shaped piece of meat (with skin intact). Chill until ready to use.

With the food processor running, drop the shallots into the work bowl and process until chopped. Add the chicken fat and continue to process until well blended. Add the cleaned shrimp, lemon juice, salt, pepper, and ½ teaspoon of the fresh thyme. Continue to process until smooth and creamy. With the machine running, slowly add the scallop juice (or stock) and whipping cream. Continue to process until the mixture resembles very thick, smooth cream. Transfer to a mixing bowl and chill (this may be done a day ahead).

Just prior to assembly, melt the butter in a medium-size skillet. Add the garlic and remaining ½ teaspoon thyme. Cook and stir 1 minute—do not let the garlic brown. Remove the skillet from the heat and add the scallops. Toss the scallops to coat with the seasoned butter. Set aside.

To assemble: Place a piece of foil on a large baking sheet. Lay the boned chicken skin side down on the foil. Lightly salt and pepper the meat. Spread the chilled shrimp mixture evenly over the meat. Remove the scallops from the seasoned butter (reserving the butter) and lay them down the middle of the roll—parallel to the long edge.

Using the foil, gently lift the longer edge of the chicken up and over the filling to meet the other side. Starting at one end, fold the end (like the flap of an envelope) to enclose the filling. Stitch together with a large needle and heavy thread. Continue to stitch the edges together, completely enclosing the filling. (*Hint*: After you have completed stitching ¾ of the roll, it will help to elevate the end of the baking sheet containing the unenclosed filling by 4″. This incline will help keep the soft filling in the sewn roll as you finish folding and stitching the open end.) When finished, you should have an oblong cylinder. Roll this off the foil and lay sewn side down on the baking sheet. Brush with the reserved seasoned butter.

Bake in a preheated 375° oven about 45 minutes, basting every 15 minutes with the pan juices. When baked, remove from the oven and let set 10 minutes before slicing. Transfer any accumulated pan juices to a small saucepan and heat. Use as a glaze for the sliced meat. Serves 6.

If you have your butcher bone the chicken, remember to specify that you want the skin left intact.

To bone the chicken yourself: Read these instructions thoroughly before beginning. If this is the first time you have boned a whole chicken, be prepared to spend 30-45 minutes completing it.

Remove the wings at the second joint. Place the chicken, breast down, on a work surface.

Using a sharp knife, split the skin down the backbone to expose the meat. Using the form of the carcass as a guide and working on one side at a time, use the tip of the knife to separate the meat from the bone. As you expose the shoulder and leg joints, you will need to cut through them to separate them from the carcass. Working down toward the breast bone, continue to separate the meat from the carcass. Repeat this process on the other side.

Cut around the wishbone end of the breast and along the breast bone to completely remove the carcass (the carcass will be in one piece). The leg, thigh, and wing bones are still in place at this point.

Lay out the chicken, skin side down, on the work surface. As you look at the chicken, the leg, thigh, and wing bones will have skin on the upper surface. Cut the exposed skin and then cut through the meat to the bone on the wing section—be careful so you do not cut all the way through to the outer skin layer. Using the tip of the knife, work the meat away from the bone and remove the bone.

In order to remove the thigh and leg bones, cut the upper skin and through the meat to expose the bone. Hold on to the tip of the drumstick and work the meat away from the bones. The leg and thigh bone should come out in one piece.

You should now have a fully boned chicken, skin intact, with (hopefully!) few holes in the skin. Use the carcass and any bones for stock.

SPICY TERIYAKI CHICKEN

On occasion we have dinner guests with diverse tastes, and we serve Spicy Teriyaki Chicken as a second entrée. It especially complements Grilled Salmon Fillets or Barbecued Spare Ribs.

6 pounds chicken thighs and legs, skinned, backbone removed and trimmed of any fat
½ cup soy sauce
¼ cup honey
2 large garlic cloves, minced
2 teaspoons minced fresh ginger root
1-2 tablespoons hot chili oil*

Combine the marinade ingredients and pour over the chicken pieces. Marinate 2-3 hours, tossing occasionally.

Transfer the marinated chicken to a baking pan just large enough to hold it, allowing a small amount of space between the pieces to ensure even baking. Spoon any remaining marinade over the chicken and bake in a preheated 375° oven 45-60 minutes. Turn the chicken every 15 minutes and baste frequently. When finished, the chicken should be a dark honey color, and the juices should run clear when the chicken is pierced with a fork. Serves 4-5.

Hot chili oil may be found on the specialty aisle in some grocery stores or in an oriental market.

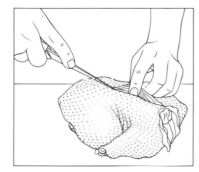

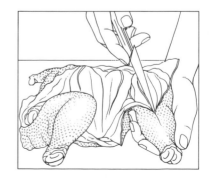

CORNISH HENS with FRUITED WILD RICE STUFFING

At the urging of Jim Van Loan and several solicitations from the company, we adapted one of our recipes designated for this book to fit an Uncle Ben's product. Here is the adaptation and the winner of the $5,000.00 Grand Prize!

½ cup whole cranberries, fresh or frozen
1 cup water
⅓ cup chopped dried apricots
1 tablespoon sugar
1 tablespoon light corn syrup
1 tablespoon dry sherry
½ cup finely chopped onion
2 garlic cloves, minced
1 tablespoon minced fresh ginger root
5 tablespoons butter
2⅔ cups chicken stock
1 6-ounce package UNCLE BEN'S™ Original Long Grain and Wild Rice
½ cup pine nuts or slivered almonds, toasted
4 Cornish game hens (about 20 ounces each), rinsed and patted dry
2 tablespoons soy sauce
1 tablespoon apricot preserves
Dried apricot halves (optional)
Parsley (optional)

Combine cranberries and water in a medium saucepan. Bring to a boil and cook 1 minute or until the skins pop. Remove from the heat and add the apricots. Let stand 1 minute. Drain, reserving the liquid. Stir the sugar, corn syrup, and sherry into the cranberries and apricots. Set aside.

Heat 2 tablespoons of the butter over medium heat and cook the onion, garlic, and ginger 1 minute. Add 2 cups of the broth and the contents of the rice to the onion mixture. Bring to a boil. Reduce heat, cover, and simmer until all liquid is absorbed, about 25 minutes. Stir the reserved fruit mixture and pine nuts into the rice.

Fill each hen cavity with approximately ½ cup rice stuffing. Skewer openings if desired. Place hens on a rack in a large, shallow roasting pan. Melt 2 tablespoons of the remaining butter, add the soy sauce and baste the hens evenly. Bake in a preheated 350° oven 1 hour or until the juices run clear when the hens are pierced with a fork. Baste every 15 minutes while the hens are cooking.

Remove the hens from the rack; keep warm. Add reserved fruit liquid and remaining ⅔ cup chicken stock to degreased pan drippings. Bring to a boil. Continue cooking to reduce by half (or until thickened as desired). Stir in the remaining 1 tablespoon butter and the apricot preserves. Serve the apricot glaze over the hens. If desired, garnish with dried apricot halves and parsley. Makes 4 servings.

Note: Any remaining stuffing may be baked in a separate dish at 350° for 20 minutes or until heated through.

SCALLOPS *in* FETA CREAM SAUCE

The delicate sweetness of the scallops and the zesty flavor of the pasta are perfect partners in this entrée.

½ cup flour
⅜ teaspoon cayenne
¼ teaspoon dried cilantro
Pinch of salt and freshly ground pepper
1 pound bay scallops
6 tablespoons butter
2 garlic cloves, finely minced
½ cup fresh cilantro leaves, loosely packed
2 cups whipping cream
3 ounces feta cheese, crumbled
1 recipe Jalapeño Pasta, cooked (page 82)

Combine the flour, cayenne, dried cilantro, salt, and pepper. Lightly dredge the scallops in the flour mixture, shaking off any excess. Melt 2 tablespoons of the butter in a heavy skillet over medium heat. Add ¼ teaspoon of the garlic and ½ of the scallops to the melted butter. Sauté 3 minutes. Remove to a heated platter. Add an additional 2 tablespoons butter, ¼ teaspoon garlic, and the remaining scallops to the skillet and sauté 3 minutes. Remove to the heated platter.

In the same skillet melt the remaining 2 tablespoons butter and add the remaining garlic. Cook 2 minutes, stirring constantly. Do not let the garlic brown. Add the fresh cilantro leaves and toss to coat. Add the whipping cream. Increase the heat. Reduce liquid until the cream starts to thicken. Add the feta cheese and stir until melted. Return the scallops and any accumulated juices to the skillet and cook just long enough to heat through.

Toss a small amount of the sauce with the cooked pasta. Arrange the pasta on 4 serving plates. Top each with an equal amount of the scallops and sauce. Serves 4.

GRILLED SALMON FILLETS

Over the years we have presented salmon to our guests in many forms. We now feel marinating and barbecuing salmon is the best way to retain its fresh flavor. The marinade and barbecuing technique we have developed is a "never-fail" method. The fish remains moist, and the fresh salmon flavor is unencumbered by rich sauce.

1 4-5 pound whole, fresh salmon, filleted
   (With head and tail on, allow about
   1 pound per person)
¼ cup vegetable oil
2 tablespoons lemon juice
3 tablespoons soy sauce
1 large garlic clove, minced
½ teaspoon dried thyme

Place the salmon fillets in a glass or other non-corrosive baking pan. Combine the oil, lemon juice, soy sauce, garlic, and thyme. Pour over the salmon fillets. Marinate 1 hour, turning the fish occasionally.

Prepare the barbecue. Cover the barbecue grate with aluminum foil. Remove the fillets from the baking pan, reserving the marinade, and place skin side down on the foil. Basting with the reserved marinade, grill the fish over medium heat 20-25 minutes, until the fish flakes easily with a fork. Do not turn the fish.

When the fillets are cooked, you should be able to transfer them to a serving platter, leaving the skin behind on the foil! Serves 4-5.

RED SNAPPER with JALAPEÑO LIME MARINADE

One evening, when preparing a red meat entrée, we had a last-minute request for fresh fish. We had experimented with variations of this marinade on pork and realized the flavors would go well with red snapper. It was an unquestioned success!

2 fresh jalapeño peppers, seeded and
    chopped*
⅓ cup chopped yellow onion
1 heaping tablespoon minced fresh
    ginger root
1 teaspoon minced fresh rosemary
1 teaspoon salt
¼ cup lime juice
¼ cup water
1½ pounds fresh red snapper fillets, bones
    removed and trimmed of any fat
½ cup Seasoned Flour (recipe follows)
2 teaspoons butter
2 teaspoons olive oil
Lime wedges (optional)

Puree the jalapeño peppers, onion, ginger, rosemary, salt, lime juice, and water to make a thick marinade. Place the trimmed fish in a noncorrosive baking pan, cover with the puree, and marinate 1-2 hours, turning occasionally.

Remove the fillets from the marinade and lightly dredge in the seasoned flour, shaking off any excess. Melt the butter and olive oil in a skillet over medium heat. Sauté the fillets 3-4 minutes per side until the fish flakes easily with a fork. Arrange on a serving platter and garnish with lime wedges. Serves 4.

When working with hot peppers, be sure to wear plastic gloves and keep your hands away from your eyes and face.

SEASONED FLOUR

½ cup flour
1¼ teaspoons dried rosemary
1¼ teaspoons dried marjoram
¼ teaspoon salt
¼ teaspoon pepper
⅛ teaspoon cayenne pepper

Combine all of the above ingredients, mixing well. This flour is easy to keep on hand as it holds well under refrigeration.

For a quick entrée, add ⅓ cup freshly grated Parmesan to the above and coat either boned chicken breast or fresh fish fillets. Sauté in butter or olive oil until done. The whole process should take less than 10-15 minutes!

GARLIC BAKED LEG of LAMB

This combination of garlic, mustard, rosemary, peppery chili sauce, and lamb has become another favorite among our guests.

1 5-pound leg of lamb, boned and trimmed
3 large cloves garlic, minced
2 tablespoons Dijon mustard
2 tablespoons soft butter
1½ teaspoons chili garlic sauce*
1 teaspoon dried rosemary

Combine the garlic, mustard, butter, chili garlic sauce, and the rosemary. Rub the unrolled leg of lamb with the garlic mixture. Fold the leg in half and place, fat side up, on a rack set in a shallow baking pan.

Roast in a preheated 425° oven for 10 minutes. Reduce the heat to 375° and continue to cook for 45 minutes. At this point, open up the leg and lay flat on the baking rack. Bake an additional 15 minutes to seal the interior meat (we allow 15 minutes per pound, total oven time, for a rare roast.) Serves 6-8.

Note: We often pull our meat a little early and let it set 15-20 minutes before carving (it will continue to cook a bit due to residual heat). This technique will produce a very moist, tender leg of lamb that is neither overdone on the outside nor too rare on the inside.

*Chili garlic sauce can be found on the specialty aisle in some grocery stores or in an oriental market.

BARBECUED LAMB CHOPS

A green salad, simple potato, and a bottle of good pinot noir, and you have dinner!

8-10 lamb chops, trimmed of any fat
½ cup red wine
2 tablespoons olive oil
1 tablespoon soy sauce
1 teaspoon lemon juice
2 garlic cloves, minced
1 teaspoon dried rosemary
½ teaspoon dried oregano
½ teaspoon salt

Place the trimmed lamb chops in a non-corrosive baking dish. Combine the red wine, olive oil, soy sauce, lemon juice, garlic, rosemary, oregano, and salt. Pour over the lamb chops. Marinate 2-4 hours, turning the chops occasionally.

Prepare the barbecue. When the coals are ready, remove the lamb chops from the marinade and place on the barbecue grill. Cook 4 minutes per side for rare. While cooking, baste with remaining marinade. Serves 4.

SEASONED LAMB *in* PHYLLO

We buy our lamb whole from a local rancher, rather than specific cuts from the butcher. As a result, we always have quite a quantity of ground lamb to work with. We have developed a number of recipes using ground lamb, but this one, reminiscent of the Middle East, is our favorite.

1¼ pounds ground lamb
1 egg
4 whole green onions, minced
½ cup minced fresh parsley
1 large garlic clove, minced
1¼ teaspoons ground cumin
½ teaspoon freshly ground pepper
Salt to taste
1 large carrot, cut in 1" julienne
½ cup butter
1 ounce pine nuts
8 small mushroom caps, sliced
1 10-ounce package frozen spinach, thawed
   and squeezed dry
2 ounces feta cheese, crumbled
⅛ teaspoon freshly grated nutmeg
Salt and freshly ground pepper to taste
2 egg whites, lightly beaten
6 sheets phyllo dough

Combine the lamb, egg, onions, parsley, garlic, cumin, pepper, and a dash of salt. Mix well. Cook a small amount of this mixture in a skillet, taste, and adjust the seasonings. Shape the remaining ground lamb mixture into 3 equal, 3"×4"×½" thick patties. Sauté in a hot skillet just long enough to sear both sides. Remove from the skillet and place on paper towels to drain and cool.

Lightly blanch the julienne carrot in boiling water until tender but crisp. Drain and immerse in ice water to stop the cooking process. Set aside on a towel to drain. Melt 1 tablespoon of the butter in a skillet and add the pine nuts. Toast lightly and remove. Melt an additional 2 tablespoons of butter and add the mushrooms. Sauté

2-3 minutes. Remove from the stove and add the carrots, pine nuts, spinach, feta cheese, nutmeg, salt, and pepper. Mix well. Taste and adjust seasonings as necessary. Fold in the egg whites.

Melt the remaining 5 tablespoons of butter in a small pan and remove from the heat. Place one sheet of phyllo dough on a work surface, brush with butter, and top with a second sheet.* Working lengthwise with the dough, place a lamb patty ¼ of the the way down from the top edge. Top with ⅓ of the spinach mixture. Fold the top edge of the pastry over the filling and brush with butter. Fold the sides inward and roll up, brushing the final fold with butter to seal. Continue with the remaining phyllo, lamb, and spinach. Place on an ungreased sheet and brush the tops with butter. Bake in a preheated 400° oven 20 minutes, until golden brown. Remove from the oven, cut in half diagonally, and serve. Serve 4-6.

Note: Cover remaining phyllo dough with a piece of saran wrap and a towel to prevent the dough from drying out. Any unused dough should be tightly wrapped and either refrigerated or frozen.

BARBECUED BEEF TENDERLOIN

A long-standing tradition at the Inn, this recipe is, without question, the entrée most often requested.

3-4 pounds trimmed beef tenderloin
2 cups 7 UP
10 tablespoons Worcestershire sauce
6 tablespoons soy sauce
1 large garlic clove, minced
1 teaspoon minced fresh ginger root
Salt and pepper

Place the trimmed tenderloin in a pan. Combine the 7 UP, Worcestershire sauce, soy sauce, garlic, and ginger. Pour over the beef tenderloin. Marinate 2-3 hours in a cool spot in the kitchen.

Prepare the barbecue. Remove the tenderloin from the pan, reserving the marinade, and place on the grill. Sear the tenderloin on all sides, and lightly salt and pepper the meat. For rare meat, continue cooking 20 minutes, frequently turning and basting the meat. Serves 6-8.

*If you are trimming your own meat, you will want to remove all the fat and shiny membrane. Remove the fat first. Then, starting at the small end of the tenderloin, slip the tip of the knife under the membrane and work it away from the meat.

BARBECUED FLANK STEAK

This flank steak will melt in your mouth as long as it has adequate time in the marinade. For best results, we suggest placing the flank in the marinade first thing in the morning. We have marinated it for as little as 3 hours and have been successful.

¼ cup soy sauce
¼ cup vegetable oil
3 tablespoons vinegar
2 tablespoons honey
1½ teaspoons garlic powder
1½ teaspoons powdered ginger
1 whole green onion, finely minced
3 pounds flank steak, trimmed*

Combine the soy sauce, oil, vinegar, honey, garlic powder, ginger, and the green onion. Mix well. Place the trimmed flank steak in a large zip-lock bag and add the marinade. Seal, releasing any air and set the bag in a larger baking pan. Turn on occasion. If preparing early in the day, place in the refrigerator.

Prepare the barbecue. Remove the meat from the bag, reserving the marinade. Place the flank steak on the grill. Sear to seal the meat. Cook 8-10 minutes per side for rare, frequently turning and basting. Remove from the grill and slice thinly across the grain. Serves 4-6.

*If you are trimming your own meat, you will want to remove all the fat and shiny membrane. Remove the fat first. Then, starting at the small end of the flank steak, slip the tip of the knife under the membrane and work it away from the meat.

MARINATED PORK TENDERLOIN with GLAZED ONIONS

Until this recipe was developed, we had several disappointments over the years with pork tenderloin drying out during cooking and had nearly abandoned preparing it. Now we have an entrée that is always sure to please our guests!

2 pork tenderloins, trimmed
   (about 3 to 3½ pounds)
¼ cup sweet rice wine*
¼ cup soy sauce
2 tablespoons rice wine vinegar*
1 tablespoon oyster sauce*
1 teaspoon sesame oil*
Several drops hot chili oil*
2 large cloves garlic, minced
1 tablespoon minced fresh ginger root
3 tablespoons honey
Glazed Onions (recipe follows)

Combine the rice wine, soy sauce, rice wine vinegar, oyster sauce, sesame oil, hot chili oil, garlic, and ginger. Mix well. Place the trimmed pork tenderloins in a large zip-lock bag and pour the marinade over them. Seal, releasing any air. Place the bag in a large pan and marinate 2-3 hours.

Reserving the marinade, remove the pork tenderloins from the bag and place them on a rack set in a shallow baking pan. Add the 3 tablespoons of honey to the reserved marinade and mix well. Brush the tenderloins with the sweetened marinade.

Pour ½" hot water into the bottom of the baking pan and set the pan in a preheated 375° oven. Bake 45-60 minutes, turning and basting the meat every 15 minutes (when finished, the center of the tenderloin should have just a hint of pink).

Remove from the oven and slice.** Arrange on a serving plate over a base of glazed onions. Serves 4-6.

*All of these ingredients may be found on the specialty aisle of some grocery stores or in an oriental market.

**The tenderloins are generally small in diameter; when we slice them, we cut across the grain at a diagonal to achieve a large slice.

◆

GLAZED ONIONS

10 tablespoons butter
4 large onions, cut in fairly large chunks
   (about 9 cups)
2 tablespoons sugar
¼ cup applejack
1 tablespoon Madeira
3 tablespoons white wine vinegar
Salt and pepper to taste

Using a large, heavy-bottomed saucepan, melt the butter over medium heat. Add the onions and toss to coat. Cook 30 minutes, until very soft, stirring occasionally. Add the sugar and cook an additional 5-10 minutes. Raise the heat and add the applejack, Madeira, and white wine vinegar. Cook, stirring constantly, for 3-4 minutes to evaporate some of the alcohol.

Remove from the heat and add salt and pepper to taste. This recipe may be done ahead and reheated just before serving. Makes 3 cups.

Note: Any leftover onion makes a wonderful base for a soup or an addition to sautéed carrots. Experiment!

Rice, Potatoes, Etc.

In the traditional "meat and potatoes" diet, served up in many of the old fishing camps along the North Umpqua River, the meat received most of the cook's attention while the potatoes provided bulk and energy for hungry fishermen. But in the modern Fisherman's Dinner, Pat and Sharon have explored a different and expanded role for these complementary dishes. And, of course, they're not just potatoes any more!

One part of that expanded role is to balance the texture of the evening's main entrée. If the entrée seems a bit on the heavy side (let's say it's Marinated Pork Tenderloin), the cooks might balance the meal with a light Walnut Rice or Mushroom Parsley Pilaf. If the entrée is lighter, perhaps a spicy Jalapeño Pasta or Cheesy Grated Potato dish is in order. (A cheesy grated potatoes serving is so hearty—combining chopped green onions and tomatoes, parsley, and bacon on a potato smothered with melted cheddar cheese—that it's been lovingly knicknamed the "Pizza Potato" by guests.)

As they've expanded these complementary dishes beyond the realm of the traditional potato, Sharon and Pat have incorporated many foods utilized by the native people and early settlers in the Umpqua Valley. Wild rice was gathered and favored by native groups. Nuts were annually harvested along the river by local people, and the cooks have used them extensively to gain more texture in their rice dishes. Rogue River blue cheese and grated Tillamook® Cheddar add a locally distinctive taste to rice, pasta or potatoes.

Served family-style and passed around the long dining room table on heaping platters during the Fisherman's Dinner, these complementary dishes evoke more than their share of appreciative comments from guests. The visitors have come to savor the North Umpqua canyon and its subtle, sylvan pleasures, rarely suspecting that part of their enjoyment might also derive from the quiet side of dinner. In the recipes that follow, another set of surprises unfolds from the Steamboat Inn!

WALNUT RICE

This recipe was developed after Sharon had a wonderful meal at a friend's home. One dish that stood out was a nutted rice. Sharon recreated the dish, which we serve with fish or chicken.

2 tablespoons butter
3 large garlic cloves, minced and divided
½ cup chopped celery
1 cup long grain white rice
2 cups chicken stock
Dash cayenne
Salt to taste (omit if using canned stock)
1 tablespoon walnut oil
½ cup chopped walnuts

Melt the butter in a saucepan and add the celery and half of the garlic. Sauté 2 minutes, add the rice, and cook an additional 3 minutes, stirring constantly. Add the stock and bring to a boil. Reduce the heat, cover, and simmer 15 minutes.

Meanwhile, heat the walnut oil in a skillet and add the remaining garlic and the walnuts. Sauté, stirring constantly, until the walnuts start to brown. Remove from the heat.

After the rice has cooked for 15 minutes, remove from the heat. Add the sautéed walnut mixture and cayenne. Taste. Add salt if necessary. Replace the lid and let set to season 5-10 minutes. Serves 4.

MUSHROOM and PARSLEY PILAF

Many of our guests stay with us for a week or more, and we design our menus to avoid repetition (unless requested!). This pilaf recipe was created to add the needed variety in our menus.

6 tablespoons butter
4 large shallots, minced
3 large garlic cloves, minced
1 pound mushrooms, caps sliced and the stems minced
1½ cups long grain white rice
3 cups chicken stock
½ teaspoon salt (omit if using canned stock)
Pepper to taste
½ cup minced fresh parsley

Melt 3 tablespoons of the butter in a saucepan. Add the shallots, garlic, and minced mushroom stems. Sauté 3 minutes, stirring constantly. Add the rice, cook, and stir until the rice begins to brown—about 5 minutes. Add the stock and bring to a boil. Reduce the heat, cover, and simmer 15-20 minutes.

Melt the remaining butter and sauté the sliced mushroom caps. Stir the parsley and sautéed mushroom caps (along with any pan juices) into the cooked rice. Taste and season with salt and pepper. Serves 6.

WILD and BROWN RICE PILAF

This is often our first choice to accompany Marinated Pork Tenderloin. The crisp texture and slightly sweet flavor are a perfect complement to the very tender pork. It also goes well with turkey, duck, and Cornish hens.

¾ cup wild rice
Boiling water
¾ cup brown rice, long or short grain
2 tablespoons butter
2 tablespoons bacon drippings
1 cup chopped celery with leaves
1 cup chopped onions
1 garlic clove, minced
3 cups apple juice
⅓ cup currants or golden raisins
⅓ cup dry sherry
½ teaspoon salt
Pepper to taste

Place the wild rice in a saucepan 1-1½ hours prior to cooking. Cover with boiling water and put a lid on the pan. Set aside. Place the currants in the sherry and set aside.

One hour before serving, melt the butter and bacon drippings in a large saucepan. Add the celery, onion, and garlic. Sauté briefly. Drain the wild rice. Add wild rice, brown rice, salt, and pepper to the sautéed vegetables. Add the apple juice and bring to a boil. Reduce the heat, cover, and simmer 40-50 minutes (check the liquid level halfway through the cooking and add water if necessary).* When finished, add the currants and sherry. Mix well. Taste and adjust as necessary. Serves 6.

If wild rice has been stored for an extended period of time, it will take longer to cook.

MUSHROOM-BARLEY CASSEROLE

We love the texture and the nutty flavor of barley and often choose it as an accompaniment to barbecued entrées. Any leftovers are a wonderful beginning for a hearty barley soup!

4 tablespoons butter
1 cup coarsely chopped onion
2 garlic cloves, minced
3 cups sliced mushroom caps
¾ cup barley
1½ cups beef or chicken stock (or water)
½ teaspoon salt
⅛ teaspoon pepper
3 tablespoons minced fresh parsley

Melt the butter in a large skillet. Add the onions and garlic. Cook 5 minutes and add the sliced mushroom caps and barley. Cook an additional 10 minutes, until the barley has started to brown. Stir in the stock, salt, and pepper and transfer to a buttered casserole dish. Bake in a preheated 375° oven for 45-60 minutes. Stir in the minced parsley. Serves 4-6.

SEASONED COUSCOUS

Couscous has become one of our favorite grains to work with. It cooks quickly and lends itself to a variety of seasonings. Couscous may be served either hot, or in a cold summer salad.

1½ cups quick cooking couscous
1 tablespoon seasoned olive oil from the
    sun-dried tomatoes
2 small garlic cloves, finely minced (about
    1½ teaspoons)
¼ pound medium mushrooms, stemmed,
    caps sliced (reserve stems for another use)
2 tablespoons sun-dried tomatoes, cut in
    ¼" dice
½ teaspoon salt
½ teaspoon minced fresh thyme (optional)
Dash cayenne pepper
2 cups rich chicken stock
2 tablespoons butter

Place the couscous in a medium-size saucepan and set aside.

Heat the seasoned oil in a medium-size skillet. Add the garlic and heat to release the flavors, but do not let brown. Add the sliced mushrooms and cook until limp. Add the diced sun-dried tomatoes, salt, thyme (optional), cayenne, and chicken stock. Simmer 1 minute to allow the tomatoes to soften. Bring to a boil and add the butter. Immediately remove from the heat and pour over the couscous. Stir, cover the pan, and set aside for 5 minutes. Remove the cover and stir with a large fork to separate the grains and fluff the couscous. The liquid should all be absorbed and the couscous softened. Serves 4-6.

THREE-PEPPER COUSCOUS

A versatile side dish! When served cold or at room temperature, it is perfect for a picnic or hot summer evening. Try it with chicken or lamb if you need something on the lighter side to round out a menu. The peppers add a dash of vivid color!

3 tablespoons olive oil
½ medium green pepper, cut into ¼" dice
½ medium red pepper, cut into ¼" dice
½ medium yellow pepper, cut into ¼" dice
1 teaspoon minced shallot (about 1 small)
¼ cup loosely packed fresh cilantro leaves,
    minced (about 1 tablespoon minced)
1 tablespoon chopped fresh chives
1½ cups quick cooking couscous
1½-1¾ cups chicken stock
2 pinches cayenne pepper

Heat the olive oil in a medium-size skillet. Add the diced peppers and the shallots. Sauté over medium heat 2-3 minutes, stirring constantly. Remove from the heat and add the chives and cilantro. Set aside.

Place the couscous in a pan that has a tight-fitting lid. Bring 1½ cups stock to a boil. Pour the boiling stock over the couscous. Stir and cover. Set aside 5 minutes. Remove the cover and stir with a large fork to separate the grains. Add the sautéed peppers. Stir and taste. If the couscous seems dry, bring the remaining stock to a boil and add it. Stir to combine. Cover the pan and let set an additional 5 minutes. Remove the cover and stir to separate the grains (if you have used home-made stock you may want to add some salt at this point). Serve warm or at room temperature. Serves 6.

JALAPEÑO PASTA

A pasta with a wonderfully distinct flavor! It was developed to accompany the Scallops in Feta Cream Sauce. It is also a heavenly addition to a summer pasta salad.

¼ cup fresh cilantro leaves
3 good-sized jalapeño peppers, cut in ¼'s
   and seeded
2 eggs, beaten
1 tablespoon olive oil
2 cups white flour
¼ teaspoon salt
1-2 tablespoons cold water (if needed)

Place the cilantro in the work bowl of a food processor and pulse 3-4 times. With the machine running, drop in the jalapeño pieces and process until chopped. Add the eggs and olive oil. Pulse until combined. Scrape down the sides of the work bowl. Combine the flour and salt. Add and process until the mixture forms a ball, adding the water, if necessary, 1 tablespoon at a time. Knead in the work bowl for 30 seconds.

By hand: Divide the dough into 2 pieces and cover with a towel. Using one piece of dough at a time, place on a floured board and flatten into a rectangle about 1" thick. Using a heavy rolling pin, roll and turn the dough until it is paper thin. If the dough sticks at any time, lift it and sprinkle some flour on the work surface. Lightly dust the rolled pasta with flour and let it rest for about 10 minutes. Gently roll the sheet of pasta up and cut it to the desired width with a sharp knife. Repeat the process with the remaining dough.

By pasta machine: Divide the dough into 3 equal pieces and cover with a towel. Set the rollers of the pasta machine as far apart as possible. Feed the dough, using one piece at a time, through the rollers. Roll the strip of dough through the first setting 3-4 times. Set the rollers down a notch and feed the dough through 2 times. Continue in

this manner until you have reached the fourth notch—dusting the pasta with flour if it seems at all sticky. Cut the pasta with the desired blade of the machine.

To cook: Drop the pasta into a pot of rapidly boiling, salted water. Cook 5-10 minutes, until just tender. Drain and toss with the sauce of your choice.

HOMEMADE PASTA

Pasta, with seemingly endless variations, provides a great accent to a memorable dinner. When you start with a homemade pasta, it takes little else to complete a meal.

1½ cups white flour
¼ teaspoon salt
4 teaspoons olive oil
2 eggs, beaten
2-4 tablespoons cold water

Combine the flour and salt in the work bowl of a food processor and pulse a couple of times. Add the olive oil and eggs. Process until well blended. With the machine running, add the cold water 1 tablespoon at a time until the dough holds together and forms a ball. Knead in the processor 30 seconds. See Jalapeño Pasta recipe, above, for instructions on rolling out and cooking pasta. Serves 4-6.

Sesame Pasta: Add 1 tablespoon toasted sesame seeds to the flour. Use 2 teaspoons sesame oil and 2 teaspoons vegetable oil as a substitute for the olive oil. Proceed as above. Sesame pasta nicely complements Marinated Pork Tenderloin or Spicy Teriyaki Chicken.

SPINACH PASTA with WALNUT SAUCE

Here is one of those seemingly endless pasta variations we mentioned earlier! The delicate Spinach Pasta and rich Walnut Sauce are sure to be a winner at your dinner table! We generally serve this with lightly seasoned chicken breasts.

1½ cups white flour
2 ounces frozen spinach, thawed and
    squeezed dry
¼ teaspoon salt
4 teaspoons olive oil
1 egg, beaten
2-4 tablespoons cold water
1 recipe Walnut Sauce (recipe follows)

With the exception of adding the spinach to the flour and salt, prepare the Spinach Pasta in the same manner as the Jalapeño Pasta (page 82).

WALNUT SAUCE

½ cup butter
1 small garlic clove, minced
1 cup finely ground toasted walnuts (about
    4 ounces)
2 cups whipping cream
½ teaspoon lemon juice
¼ teaspoon freshly ground pepper
¼ teaspoon freshly ground nutmeg
Dash salt

Melt the butter in a skillet and add the garlic. Cook, stirring constantly, until the garlic starts to soften, about 3 minutes. Add the ground walnuts, whipping cream, and lemon juice to the pan. Raise the heat and simmer, stirring often, until it starts to thicken. When thickened, remove from the heat and add the pepper, nutmeg, and dash of salt. Mix well. Makes 2¼ cups sauce. Toss with the Spinach Pasta and serve. Serves 4-6.

CHEESY GRATED POTATOES

The complementary flavors of the potato, cheese, bacon, and herbs make this recipe a hit with young and old. If you are lucky enough to have some left after dinner, it reheats easily and is tasty with breakfast or brunch.

¾ pound bacon
3 pounds potatoes, peeled
½ pound Swiss cheese, grated
¼ cup freshly grated Parmesan cheese
3 garlic cloves, minced
2-3 teaspoons dried basil
6 whole green onions, minced
¼ cup minced fresh parsley
6-8 tablespoons butter, melted
¼ pound Cheddar cheese, grated
3 small tomatoes, seeded and diced
Salt and pepper to taste

Chop the bacon and fry until crisp. Drain on paper towels and set aside.

Boil the potatoes until tender. Drain and chill. When the potatoes are cold, grate them and place in a large bowl. Add ½ of the Swiss cheese, the Parmesan cheese, minced garlic, basil, ½ of the green onions, 1 tablespoon parsley, and ¼ cup melted butter. Mix well. If the mixture seems at all dry, add a little more butter. Lightly pat onto a buttered 12″ × 18″ baking sheet. Top with the bacon, remaining green onions, remaining parsley, tomatoes, Swiss and Cheddar cheese. Drizzle with 2-3 tablespoons melted butter. Bake in a preheated 350° oven 20 minutes, until the cheese is melted and the potatoes are heated through. Serves 8-10.

POTATO *and* VEGETABLE PANCAKES

The vegetables and herbs in this recipe add additional flavors and texture to the classic French potato pancake.

6 tablespoons butter
1 cup coarsely chopped mushrooms
3 small leeks, use white part only, cut in
 ½" julienne
2 garlic cloves, minced
1 teaspoon dried thyme
1 teaspoon dried basil
¼ teaspoon salt
Dash pepper
6 ounces cream cheese, room temperature
2 tablespoons flour
2 eggs, beaten
6 ounces dry Monterey Jack cheese, diced
 small
½ pound zucchini
1½ pounds potatoes
2-4 tablespoons cream (optional)

━━━

Melt 3 tablespoons of the butter in a large skillet. Add the mushrooms, leeks, garlic, thyme, basil, salt, and pepper. Cook until all of the liquid has evaporated. Set aside to cool.

Combine the cream cheese, flour, beaten eggs, and diced dry Monterey Jack cheese.

Cut the zucchini in fourths lengthwise, remove and discard the pith, and grate coarsely. Squeeze in a towel to remove any excess moisture.

Peel the potatoes and grate coarsely. Squeeze in a towel to remove any excess moisture.

Combine the mushroom and cheese mixtures with the zucchini and potatoes. If the mixture seems too thick, add a couple of tablespoons of the cream. Cook a small amount of the mixture to test the seasonings. Adjust as necessary. Using a ⅓- to ½-cup measure, ladle the pancakes onto a buttered grill or into a skillet with melted butter. Cook over medium heat for 2-3 minutes per side, until golden brown and the potatoes are cooked through. Serves 6.

SOY-SESAME POTATOES

Do not let the simplicity of this recipe mislead you! The finished dish is very full-flavored and an excellent addition to a menu featuring a barbecued entrée.

2 pounds red potatoes*
½ cup butter, melted
¼ cup soy sauce
3-4 tablespoons sesame seeds

━━━

Combine the butter and soy sauce.** Brush a baking sheet with melted butter. Cut the potatoes lengthwise into ⅜" slices, and then cut those slices into ⅜" strips. Without crowding them together, place the potatoes on the buttered baking sheet. Brush with the soy butter and sprinkle with the sesame seeds. Bake in a preheated 375° oven 40 minutes. Serves 4.

If you do not have red potatoes on hand, white potatoes will work. We prefer the sweetness the red potatoes add to the finished dish.

**Any remaining soy butter will hold well when tightly covered and refrigerated.*

HERBED PARMESAN POTATOES

A quick scan of this recipe's ingredients may not spawn the interest it deserves, but do not pass it by! The accent of the herbs and cheese on a lightly buttered potato is very pleasing.

6 tablespoons butter, melted
2 pounds red potatoes
2-3 teaspoons dried basil*
¼ cup freshly grated Parmesan cheese

Cut the potatoes lengthwise into ½" thick slices. Without crowding the slices, place on a buttered baking sheet. Brush the tops of the slices with melted butter and sprinkle with the basil. Top with Parmesan cheese and a drizzling of melted butter. Bake in a preheated 375° oven 45 minutes. Serves 6.

*We often use rosemary or another herb, depending on what accompanies the potatoes.

ROSEMARY-BLUE CHEESE POTATOES

This is a recipe we developed with lamb in mind and were very pleased with its pairing with the lamb. The sweet red potatoes gracefully take on the soft accent of the blue cheese.

1½ pounds red potatoes, cut in ½" cubes
2 tablespoons butter
2 tablespoons blue cheese
1 teaspoon minced fresh rosemary
2 tablespoons minced fresh parsley
Dash of salt, pepper, and cayenne

Cook the potatoes 10 minutes in a pot of rapidly boiling, salted water. Drain and set aside.

Melt the butter and blue cheese and add the rosemary. Combine the partially cooked potatoes and the butter mixture and place on an ungreased baking sheet. Bake in a preheated 375° oven 20-25 minutes. Remove from the oven and sprinkle with the parsley, salt, pepper, and cayenne. Mix well. Serves 6.

MUSHROOM SOUFFLÉ

On occasion we use a soufflé as a substitute for the starch course in our menus. We may be trying to lighten up a menu or to achieve a flavor or texture only a soufflé can lend. This soufflé is suited to heartier entrées such as Barbecued Beef Tenderloin.

½ pound mushrooms, finely minced
1 tablespoon minced shallots
6 tablespoons butter
3 tablespoons flour
1 cup milk
¾ teaspoon salt
¼ teaspoon pepper
Dash cayenne and freshly grated nutmeg
4 egg yolks, room temperature
5 egg whites, room temperature
1 cup coarsely grated Swiss cheese
2 tablespoons freshly grated Parmesan
  cheese

Place the mushrooms in a kitchen towel (not terry cloth) and twist it to remove any excess moisture. Melt 3 tablespoons of the butter. Add the mushrooms, shallots, and ¼ teaspoon salt. Cook 5 minutes. Set aside.

Melt 3 tablespoons butter in a large saucepan and stir in the flour. Cook until thick and bubbly. Remove from the heat and slowly stir in the milk until well blended. Add the remaining ½ teaspoon salt, the pepper, cayenne, and nutmeg. Mix well. Return to the heat and bring to a boil and cook 1 minute, stirring constantly. Remove from the heat and beat in the egg yolks one at a time—making sure the first is incorporated before adding the next. Combine the egg yolk mixture with the mushrooms.

Beat the egg whites and a pinch of salt until stiff but not dry. Stir ¼ of the whites and the Swiss cheese into the egg yolk sauce. Gently fold in the remaining egg whites. Pour into a soufflé dish that has been buttered and dusted with 1 tablespoon of the Parmesan cheese. Top with the remaining Parmesan cheese. Place in a preheated 400° oven. Immediately reduce the heat to 375° and bake 30-45 minutes. Remove from the oven and serve immediately. Serves 6.

GREEN CHILI and CORN SOUFFLÉ

We like this soufflé in combination with the Red Snapper with Jalapeño Lime Marinade. It is also good with corned beef or a glazed ham.

2 tablespoons butter
1 tablespoon flour
¼ cup cornmeal
½ cup chicken stock
4 egg yolks, room temperature
½ cup sour cream
¼ pound jalapeño jack cheese, grated
10 ounces whole kernel corn, fresh or
   frozen*
2 tablespoons minced green chilies, drained
   on paper towels
1 tablespoon minced green onion
¾ teaspoon salt
Dash cayenne
5 egg whites, room temperature
¼ teaspoon cream of tartar

Melt the butter in a saucepan and stir in the flour and cornmeal. Cook until bubbly. To avoid any lumps, stir in the stock slowly. Cook, stirring constantly, until thickened. Remove from the heat and beat in the egg yolks, one at a time, making sure the first is incorporated before adding the next. Add the sour cream, grated cheese, whole corn, drained green chilies, green onion, salt, and cayenne.

Mix thoroughly. Beat the egg whites with the cream of tartar until stiff but not dry. Stir ¼ of the whites into the corn base. Gently fold in the remaining whites and pour into a buttered soufflé dish. Place the dish in a preheated 400° oven. Immediately reduce the heat to 375° and bake for 40-45 minutes until set. Remove from the oven and serve immediately. Serves 4-6.

*If using frozen corn, lay out on a paper towel to absorb the ice crystals while you are preparing other ingredients.

HERBED CARROT RING

This recipe is used as a replacement for a rice, pasta, or potato when the menu needs a lighter touch. The ring is an attractive presentation when filled with bright green, stir-fried vegetables.

2 pounds carrots, peeled and cut into
    ½" chunks
3 tablespoons butter
3 tablespoons flour
½ cup milk
3 eggs, separated
½ teaspoon salt
½ teaspoon tarragon
1 tablespoon minced fresh parsley
Pinch of garlic powder and white pepper
4-cup ring mold

Bring a 4-quart pot of water to a boil. Add a pinch of salt and the carrots. Cook until tender but not soft. Drain and let set 5 minutes. Transfer to the work bowl of a food processor and pulse until chopped but not pureed. (The carrots should still have some texture to them but should not be in large chunks.) Transfer to a mixing bowl and set aside.

Melt the butter in a small saucepan. Add the flour and cook until bubbly. Slowly stir in the milk and continue to cook until thickened. Add the salt, tarragon, parsley, garlic powder, and white pepper. Stir in the egg yolks, one at a time, making sure the first is incorporated before adding the next. Add to the carrots and mix well.

Beat the egg whites until stiff but not dry and stir ¼ of them into the carrot mixture. Gently fold in the remaining whites and pour into a well-buttered ring mold. Bake in a boiling water bath in a preheated 350° oven for 40-50 minutes. Serves 6.

Vegetables

What can you do with vegetables? We all know they're good for us—after all, Mother's mission in life was to get us to eat them—but every chef's challenge is to get us to enjoy them. Better yet, to exclaim over them and rave about them to our friends.

Over the years, Pat and Sharon's vegetable dishes in the Fisherman's Dinner have passed the test with flying colors—and part of the reason is the cooks' own flair for color. Picture fresh, crisp carrots, cooked lightly in raspberry vinegar—or perhaps you prefer your color combinations in medley? Try Zucchini and Three-Pepper Stir-Fry or Broccoli with Roma Tomatoes and Jicama for pizzazz.

Sharon and Pat's penchant for experimentation has resulted in a variety of vegetable dishes. In addition to combining colors, they love to liven up a meal with unpredictable combinations of vegetable textures. When it comes time to plan the week's menus, vegetables provide flexibility, and the combinations are as ever-changing as the menus that incorporate them. They're willing to wager you've never had asparagus, snow peas, mushrooms, and onions together. Or cabbage with ham and pumpkin seeds. When the vegetable platter is passed around during the Fisherman's Dinner, be prepared to try something new!

Even confirmed non-vegetable eaters have become converts at the Steamboat Inn. The same summer sun that beckons guests to the swimming holes up Steamboat Creek also ripens a plethora of garden vegetables in the Umpqua Valley for Pat and Sharon's use in their creative concoctions. They may be far from the bustling produce markets in the big cities, but in summer they have a wealth of crisp, fresh garden vegetables to combine into new dishes as their fancy dictates. Even in winter, when they must cope with their isolation and the fluctuating number of evening diners, they've learned to utilize what's on hand in new and exciting ways.

So pass the vegetables at the Steamboat Inn—don't pass them up—even though they are good for you!

ASPARAGUS, SNOW PEA, and MUSHROOM STIR-FRY

Crisp and colorful—a perfect choice for the center of the Herbed Carrot Ring.

1 pound asparagus, trimmed and cut
    diagonally into 1" pieces
5 ounces pea pods, stringed
2 teaspoons vegetable oil
½ cup thinly sliced onion
½ pound mushrooms, stemmed and
    quartered (reserve stems for another use)
2 tablespoons dry sherry
2 teaspoons soy sauce
1 tablespoon oyster sauce
1 tablespoon sugar
Dash salt and pepper
1½ teaspoons cornstarch dissolved in
    1 tablespoon cold water

Blanch the asparagus in rapidly boiling salted water for 2 minutes. Drain and immerse in ice water to stop the cooking process. Drain again and set aside.

Blanch the snow peas in rapidly boiling salted water for 30 seconds and proceed as above.

Heat the oil in a medium-sized skillet and add the onions. Cook, stirring constantly, about 3 minutes. Add the mushrooms and sherry, and cook an additional 3 minutes. Add the asparagus, snow peas, soy sauce, oyster sauce, sugar, salt, and pepper. Mix well. Continue to stir until the vegetables are cooked and heated through, about 3 more minutes. Add the cornstarch mixture and cook until vegetables are glazed. Taste and adjust the seasonings. Serves 4.

STEAMED BROCCOLI with GINGER-SESAME SEED BUTTER

A light, oriental accent for broccoli or asparagus. If you entertain often, the butter mixture is easy to keep on hand as it stores well when tightly covered and refrigerated.

1 bunch broccoli, cut into long spears and
    peeled (reserve stem end for another use)
3 tablespoons butter
2 tablespoons sesame seeds
1 teaspoon minced fresh ginger root

Lightly salt a pot of water and bring to a boil. Cook the broccoli until bright green and crisp.

Meanwhile, melt the butter in a small skillet and add the sesame seeds and fresh ginger. Cook and stir until the seeds are toasted—do not let the ginger brown.

Drain the broccoli and arrange on a serving platter. Sprinkle with salt and pepper, and drizzle with the sesame seed butter. Serves 4.

BROCCOLI with ROMA TOMATOES and JICAMA

A colorful medley of vegetables that will brighten any dinner table.

1 bunch broccoli
1 tablespoon olive oil
1 small onion, thinly sliced
1 garlic clove, minced
2 teaspoons dried basil
Large pinch of cayenne
1 cup chicken stock
8 ounces jicama, cut in 1" julienne
3 ripe Roma tomatoes, each cut into 4-6
    wedges
2 tablespoons freshly grated Parmesan
    cheese

Cut the flowerets off of the bunch of broccoli, leaving them 2½" long. Cut each of the flowerets into a bite-sized piece. Blanch in lightly salted, simmering water. Remove while still crisp and bright green. Immerse in ice water to stop the cooking process. Drain and set aside. Peel the remaining broccoli stems and slice diagonally into ¼" slices.

Heat the olive oil in a medium-sized, heavy-bottomed skillet. Add the onions and minced garlic, stirring to combine. Add a little stock and cook until the onions soften, about 2 minutes. (Throughout the cooking process, add a little stock as the liquid in the pan concentrates.)

Add the basil, cayenne and the sliced broccoli stems. Cook until they begin to soften, but are still crisp, about 1-2 minutes. Add the jicama and stir until heated through. Then add the broccoli flowerets and stir gently until heated. Taste for seasoning and adjust at this point.* Finally, add the tomatoes and Parmesan cheese and toss gently just until combined. Serve immediately. Serves 4-6.

*If you are using canned stock, no salt will be needed as the stock will have concentrated during cooking. With homemade stock, you may need to add some salt.

BRUSSEL SPROUTS and CARROTS with ROSEMARY

As the fall colors appear on the North Umpqua, our thoughts drift toward heartier winter fare. Combining carrots with the brussel sprouts gives this dish improved color, sweetness, and texture. The rosemary complements both vegetables.

3 tablespoons butter
¼ cup thinly sliced onion
¾ pound carrots, diagonally sliced, ¼" thick
¾ pound brussel sprouts, trimmed
½ cup chicken stock
½ teaspoon dried rosemary
1-2 teaspoons sugar
Salt and pepper to taste

Melt the butter in a medium-sized skillet over medium heat. Add the onions and cook until they start to soften, about 2 minutes. Add the carrots and brussel sprouts, and toss to coat with the butter. Add the chicken stock and rosemary. Cover and cook, stirring occasionally, until the vegetables are tender, about 10-15 minutes. Add the sugar and season to taste with the salt and pepper. Serves 4-6.

HONEY MUSTARD CARROTS

The pungent mustard and sweet honey make an interesting glaze on the carrots.

2 tablespoons butter
2 tablespoons minced shallots
1 pound carrots, julienne or diagonally
  sliced
¼ cup dry white wine
2 tablespoons honey
1 tablespoon Dijon mustard
1 tablespoon chopped chives

Melt the butter in a non-corrosive saucepan. Add the shallots and carrots, and cook 5 minutes. Add the wine and cook 10 minutes until the carrots are tender but crisp and the liquid is nearly evaporated. Add the honey and mustard, cooking an additional 5 minutes. Toss in the chives and serve. Serves 4.

CARROTS with SHALLOTS and THYME

We serve this with steamed broccoli spears to add another color to the serving platter. Or, as a way of extending amounts when we have late additions to our dinner reservations!

1 tablespoon olive oil
¼ cup minced shallots
1 pound carrots, *coarsely* grated (about 5
  cups)
¼ cup chicken stock
1 teaspoon dried thyme
2-3 teaspoons sugar
2 tablespoons minced fresh parsley
Salt and pepper to taste

Heat the olive oil and add the shallots and carrots. Stir to combine. Add the stock and thyme, and cook until the carrots are softened, about 6 minutes. Add the sugar (amount depends on sweetness of the carrots), salt, and pepper. Toss in the parsley and serve. Serves 4-6.

SAUTÉED CARROTS with RASPBERRY VINEGAR

After we discovered, and began making, raspberry vinegar, we tried it in everything! This recipe is one we have come back to time after time. The sweet-tart finish on the carrots makes a good side dish for grilled meats.

2 tablespoons butter
½ cup thinly sliced onion
2 garlic cloves, minced
1 pound carrots, julienne or diagonally
  sliced
½ cup chicken stock
1 tablespoon sugar
½ teaspoon salt
2-3 tablespoons Raspberry Vinegar (page 56)
1 teaspoon cornstarch dissolved in
  2 teaspoons cold water
2 tablespoons minced fresh parsley or chives
  (for garnish)

Melt the butter in a non-corrosive saucepan. Add the onion and garlic, and cook until soft but not brown. Add the carrots and toss to coat. Add the stock, cover, and cook 10-15 minutes until the carrots are tender but crisp. Add the sugar, salt, and raspberry vinegar (amount dependent on vinegar's strength and fruitiness). Cook 2-3 minutes. Add the dissolved cornstarch and cook until the vegetables are glazed. Garnish with the parsley or chives. Serves 4.

GRATED CABBAGE and CARROTS with FILBERTS

The filberts add an interesting texture and the vermouth a subtle and surprising background flavor in this vegetable combination.

4 tablespoons butter
1 cup thinly sliced onion
3 medium carrots, *coarsely* grated
12 ounces green cabbage, thinly sliced
¼ cup dry vermouth
1 tablespoon sugar
½ cup coarsely chopped, toasted filberts
2 tablespoons minced fresh parsley
Salt and pepper to taste

Melt the butter in a large saucepan and add the onion. Cook 1 minute and add the carrots and cabbage. Toss to combine and cook 3 minutes. Add the vermouth and sugar and continue to cook 5 minutes. Add the filberts and parsley, stirring to combine. Add salt and pepper to taste. Serves 6.

SLICED CABBAGE and JULIENNE BEETS

This dish is colorful and slightly sweet—a pleasant accent to pork or poultry.

4 tablespoons butter
2 tablespoons minced shallots
1 cup cooked beets, cut in 1" julienne
1 teaspoon cornstarch
¼ cup apple juice concentrate
2 teaspoons white wine vinegar
¼ teaspoon dried dill weed
½ pound green cabbage, thinly sliced
2-3 teaspoons sugar (optional)
Salt and pepper

Melt half the butter in a non-corrosive skillet. Add half the shallots and sauté briefly. Toss in the beets and stir until heated through. Dissolve the cornstarch in the apple juice concentrate and add, along with the vinegar and dill, to the skillet. Cook and stir until bubbling and thickened. Remove to a heated plate.

Using the same skillet, sauté the remaining shallots in the remaining butter. Add the cabbage and cook until it just begins to soften and becomes translucent, about 4 minutes. Return the beets to the skillet and toss to combine. Taste and add the sugar, salt, and pepper to taste. Serves 4.

NAPA CABBAGE with HAM and PUMPKIN SEEDS

Put a surprise in a winter menu! The smoky, sweet ham and whole pumpkin seeds add interesting flavor and texture.

1 teaspoon butter
1 garlic clove, minced
3 ounces whole pumpkin seeds
1 tablespoon peanut oil*
1 pound napa cabbage, cut diagonally into
    2" strips
⅔ cup chicken stock
¼ cup light cream (half-and-half)
3 ounces ham, cut in small dice

━━━

Melt the butter and sauté the garlic and pumpkin seeds until the seeds begin to pop, stirring constantly so the garlic does not brown. Set aside.

Heat the peanut oil in a non corrosive pan. Add the cabbage and toss, cooking 2 minutes. Increase the heat and add the stock and light cream. Cook until reduced and thickened. Reduce the heat. Add the ham and reserved seeds, and stir until heated through. Taste and adjust. Serves 4.

If unavailable, use vegetable or olive oil.

CAULIFLOWER, SNOW PEA and BLACK MUSHROOM STIR-FRY

A vegetable dish with an oriental influence. The cauliflower and black mushroom are both strong-flavored vegetables and should not be combined with a delicate entrée.

1 pound cauliflower, separated into bite-
    sized flowerets
½ pound (8 ounces) snow peas, stringed
2 ounces dried black mushrooms, softened*
2 tablespoons vegetable oil
¾ cup thinly sliced onion
1 garlic clove, minced
1 teaspoon minced fresh ginger root
½ cup mushroom soaking liquid, strained to
    remove the fine grit
2 tablespoons soy sauce
1½ teaspoons cornstarch, dissolved in
    1 tablespoon cold water

━━━

Bring a pot of lightly salted water to a boil and blanch the cauliflower 8-10 minutes. Drain and immerse in ice water to stop the cooking process. Drain again and set aside.

Lightly blanch the snow peas for 30 seconds and proceed as above.

Reserving the liquid, drain the softened mushrooms. Remove the stems and discard them. Slice the caps and set aside.

Heat the oil in a large saucepan. Add the onion, garlic, and fresh ginger. Sauté 2 minutes, stirring constantly, so they do not brown. Add the cauliflower, sliced black mushrooms, ½ cup of the reserved soaking liquid, and the soy sauce. Raise the heat to high and cook five minutes. Add the snow peas and dissolved cornstarch. Continue to cook until the peas are warm and the vegetables glazed. Serves 4-6.

To soften dried mushrooms, place them in a bowl and cover with boiling water. Let set at least 30 minutes, until softened.

CAULIFLOWER *with* SUN-DRIED TOMATOES

Sun-dried tomatoes and sliced green onion liven up the bland appearance of cauliflower.

1 pound cauliflower, separated into bite-
  sized flowerets
8 slices sun-dried tomatoes packed in garlic/
  basil olive oil
1 tablespoon seasoned oil from the tomatoes
2 garlic cloves, minced
2 tablespoons thickly sliced green onion tops
⅓ cup chicken stock
¼ teaspoon salt (if using unsalted stock)
Dash cayenne

Blanch the cauliflower in lightly salted water 10 minutes. Drain and immerse in ice water to stop the cooking process. Drain again and set aside.

Cut the sun-dried tomatoes into ¼" dice. Set aside.

Heat the 1 tablespoon oil in a medium-sized skillet. Add the garlic and sauté until softened. Add the diced tomatoes and chicken stock. Bring to a boil, reduce the heat, and simmer 2 minutes to soften the tomatoes and blend the flavors. Add the cauliflower and toss to combine. Cook an additional 5 minutes. Add the green onion and season with the salt if needed and a dash of cayenne. Serves 4.

GREEN BEAN *and* MUSHROOM STIR-FRY

Vegetable medleys are often the order of the day for the evening meal. Some of the vegetable combinations "feel" right and we develop them into recipes such as this one.

2 tablespoons olive oil
½ cup thinly sliced onion
2 garlic cloves, minced
1¼ pounds frozen whole green beans*
½ pound mushrooms, stemmed and
  quartered (reserve stems for another use)
4 teaspoons dried basil
3 tablespoons soy sauce
¾ teaspoon salt
¼ teaspoon pepper
2 tablespoons dry sherry
¼ cup chicken stock
2 teaspoons cornstarch, dissolved in
  4 teaspoons water
3 medium, ripe tomatoes, cut in wedges
  (Romas work well in the winter months)
3 tablespoons freshly grated Parmesan
  cheese

Heat the oil in a large skillet. Add the onion and garlic, and toss briefly. Add the green beans, mushrooms, basil, soy sauce, salt, pepper, dry sherry, and stock. Cover and cook until the beans are heated through, about 8 minutes stirring occasionally. Add the dissolved cornstarch and heat until thickened. Toss in the tomato wedges and Parmesan cheese, stirring just to combine. Serve immediately. Serves 4-6.

*During our "off-season" we never know from one day to the next whether we will have 2 or 10 for dinner. Since we are forty miles from the nearest large market, we try to keep products on hand that can easily be converted into an interesting vegetable dish—such as good quality frozen whole green beans, peas, or spinach.

ZUCCHINI and THREE PEPPER STIR-FRY

One couldn't ask for a brighter display of color! The simple seasonings allow the natural flavors of the vegetables to come through.

1 tablespoon olive oil
¾ cup thinly sliced red onion
1 small garlic clove, minced
½ large red pepper, seeded and cut into
    ¼" strips
½ large yellow pepper, seeded and cut into
    ¼" strips
½ large green pepper, seeded and cut into
    ¼" strips
1 tablespoon butter
1 pound zucchini, cut into ¼" diagonal
    slices*
8 medium-sized mushrooms, stemmed and
    quartered (reserve stems for another use)
¼ cup dry white wine
2 tablespoons sugar
¼ teaspoon salt
Dash pepper
1½ teaspoons cornstarch, dissolved in
    1 tablespoon cold water

———

Heat the olive oil in a medium-sized skillet. Add ½ of the onion and garlic. Add the sliced peppers and sauté 3-4 minutes, until the peppers start to soften. Remove the peppers from the skillet and set on a heated platter. Melt the butter in the same skillet. Add the remaining onion and garlic, the zucchini, mushrooms, and white wine. Cook 5 minutes and return the peppers to the pan along with the sugar, salt, and a sprinkling of pepper. Cook an additional 5 minutes.

Add the dissolved cornstarch and cook until the vegetables are glazed. Serve immediately. Serves 4.

When using zucchini (or yellow squash) in stir fries, we always remove the pithy interior. If left in, the pith will turn mushy and add a muddied look to your finished dish. We cut the zucchini lengthwise into fourths and scrape away (and discard) the very center, then slice the remainder.

———

MADEIRA MUSHROOMS

On fall evenings we often end up with a dinner table of hungry fishermen. Often they skip lunch and stay on the stream all day, knowing we will feed them a hearty dinner at dusk. When this happens, we realize our ½ pound per person of Barbequed Beef Tenderloin may not go far enough, and we start looking for ways to extend it. This rich dish often comes to mind as a topping for the beef.

6 tablespoons butter
2 large garlic cloves, minced
1 medium shallot, minced
1 pound mushrooms, stemmed and sliced
    (reserve stems for another use)
6 tablespoons Madeira
¼ teaspoon salt
Dash pepper

———

Melt the butter in a large skillet. Add the garlic and shallot, and sauté 1 minute, stirring constantly. Add the mushrooms, Madeira, salt, and a sprinkling of pepper. Cook until the mushrooms start to soften and the liquid has reduced slightly. Taste and serve hot over meat or steamed broccoli.

SPICY EGGPLANT and GREEN BEANS

We are always looking for new ways to add color and interest to eggplant as it can be rather bland in its taste and appearance. The oriental accent and the spiciness add interest; the green beans and red pepper add needed color. If you are not overly fond of spicy foods, you may want to reduce the amount of hot chili oil the first time you prepare this dish—it is always easier to add than to subtract a seasoning!

3 tablespoons vegetable oil
1½ teaspoons hot chili oil
2 garlic cloves, minced
1½ teaspoons finely minced fresh
   ginger root
1½ cups thinly sliced yellow onion
¾ pound eggplant, peeled and cut into
   ½" cubes
1 pound frozen whole green beans
½ large red pepper, cut into ¼" dice
1¼ cups chicken stock
2 tablespoons sesame oil
3 tablespoons soy sauce
2 tablespoons sweet rice wine*
1 tablespoon sugar

Heat the vegetable oil and ½ teaspoon of the hot chili oil in a large skillet. Add the garlic, ginger, onion, and eggplant, tossing to combine. Cook 2 minutes, stirring constantly. Add 1 cup of the chicken stock and cook 10 minutes over medium heat until the eggplant softens. Stir occasionally. While the eggplant is cooking, place the green beans in a heat-proof mixing bowl. Bring 4 cups water to a boil and pour over the green beans. Let set 1 minute, then drain.

Mix together the remaining 1 teaspoon hot chili oil, the sesame oil, soy sauce, remaining chicken stock, sweet rice wine, and sugar. Add, along with the green beans and red pepper, to the eggplant. Toss to combine. Continue to cook an additional 5 minutes until heated through and the seasonings have blended with the vegetables. Serves 6-8.

*See glossary.

SPAGHETTI SQUASH with DICED TOMATOES

Many times the simplest of preparations produces the most satisfying results!

1 tablespoon butter
½ cup chopped onion
3 cups cooked spaghetti squash
1 cup diced ripe seeded tomato (Romas will
   work in the winter months)

Heat the butter in a heavy-bottomed skillet. Add the onions and sauté until softened, stirring constantly, about 5 minutes. Add the spaghetti squash and stir for 5 minutes. Add the tomatoes and continue to cook an additional 5-10 minutes, until heated through. Serves 4.

Breads

The Fisherman's Dinner is served family style at the long sugar pine table in the Steamboat Inn. Dishes pass from hand to hand, pausing just long enough for each guest to select a warm slice of bread or scoop a heaping mound of vegetables onto a plate. Passing the food reminds some guests of the family dinners of their youth; others remember large family reunions or summers at camp. Serving the meal family style is a tradition that reinforces feelings of community, of family connections, just what the Van Loans intend. Their motto for the Steamboat Inn, "You are a stranger here but once," sums up their goal: Once guests join the Steamboat family, they become life members.

One of the first dishes passed around the table is the bread. Often the aroma arrives first. Perhaps it's a hint of dill, wafting out of the kitchen. Or a breath of chives as the bread basket is passed, tantalizing guests on the opposite side of the table. Then, finally, the bread basket arrives. The smell and texture of warm bread—is there anything more likely to transport us back to childhood?

In the early days at the Inn, the small kitchen limited bread baking. Because the oven was often needed for the preparation of other courses, breads which required a long baking time or took up too much space in the oven were impractical. So Pat and Sharon evolved bread recipes that were quick and easy, incorporating many of the fresh herbs from the garden and local cheeses to add distinctive flavors and variety. And the old standby of camp cooks along the river, sourdough, was elevated to new heights by creative hands at the bread board.

Grandma's Bread, a long-time favorite at Steamboat Inn, combines such diverse ingredients as scotch oats, sunflower seeds, and whole wheat flour into a tasty round loaf that gets its shape from the coffee cans in which it is baked. Guests enjoyed Grandma's Bread so much, they began to request it with their breakfast, as toast. Thus began another tradition at the Inn.

At the Steamboat Inn, bread is no afterthought. Bread supports the meal in the same way sturdy wooden wading staffs support the fishermen as they wade the swift currents of the North Umpqua. For Pat and Sharon, their bread is the strong foundation of the Fisherman's Dinner.

❖

HERB-CHEESE BREAD

Our first herb-cheese bread was developed when we had some overly ripe blue cheese. We were pleased with the results and began to try different cheese-and-herb combinations. This is one we put on the menu often.

1½ cups oats
2 teaspoons salt
2¼ teaspoons dried rosemary
1 teaspoon dried marjoram
½ teaspoon dried dill weed
¼ teaspoon garlic powder
3 tablespoons honey
¼ cup soft butter
1 cup boiling water
½ cup warm water
2 tablespoons dry yeast
2 eggs, beaten
½ cup milk
½ cup sour cream
¾ pound sharp Cheddar cheese, grated
2 cups whole wheat flour
4-5 cups white flour

Combine the oats, salt, rosemary, marjoram, dill, garlic powder, honey, and soft butter in a large mixing bowl. Add the boiling water and stir. Cool about 10 minutes until lukewarm.

Dissolve the yeast in the warm water and set aside 5-10 minutes.

Add the beaten eggs, milk, sour cream, Cheddar cheese, and whole wheat flour to the lukewarm oat mixture. Add the dissolved yeast and stir. Gradually add the white flour until you have a firm dough. Turn onto a floured board and knead until smooth and elastic. Add flour as needed to prevent the dough from sticking. Place in a greased bowl, turning the dough to coat it with oil. Cover and set in a warm place to rise until doubled in bulk, about 1 to 1½ hours.

Punch down the dough and divide into 1¼-pound loaves. Knead to shape and place in greased 4"×6" loaf pans.* Let rise until doubled in bulk.

Bake in a preheated 375° oven about 30-35 minutes. Remove from pans, place on cooling rack, and let rest 10 minutes before cutting.

*The 4"×6" bread pans produce a small-sized loaf that we feel fits our dinner baskets well. Large, sandwich-sized slices have a tendency to hang over the edges and tear. We also like the appearance of the small slice on the dinner plate.

WALNUT-ONION BREAD

A wonderful bread for a menu needing additional texture.

2 tablespoons butter
1½ cups chopped onion
1 garlic clove, minced
⅔ cup milk
¾ cup coarsely chopped toasted walnuts
2½ teaspoons salt*
1 tablespoon yeast
⅔ cup warm water
1½ cups whole wheat flour
3½-4½ cups white flour

Melt the butter in a medium-sized skillet. Add the onion and garlic, and sauté until limp but not brown. Add the milk, walnuts, and salt. Set aside to cool.

Dissolve the yeast in the warm water and set aside 5-10 minutes.

Place the cooled milk mixture in a large mixing bowl. Add the dissolved yeast and the whole wheat flour. Gradually add the white flour until you have a firm dough. Turn onto a floured board and knead until smooth and elastic. Add flour as needed to prevent the dough from sticking. Place in a greased bowl, turning the dough to coat it with oil. Cover and set in a warm place to rise until doubled in bulk, about 1 to 1½ hours.

Punch down the dough and divide into 1¼-pound loaves. Knead to shape and place in greased 4"×6" loaf pans. Let rise until doubled in bulk.

Bake in a preheated 375° oven about 30-35 minutes. Remove from pans, place on cooling rack, and let rest 10 minutes before cutting.

*When making this bread in a larger batch, cut back on the amount of salt, but double or triple the remaining ingredients.

SPICY CORNMEAL BREAD

Due to a fondness for the flavor and texture of cornmeal, we went through a period of trying it in many dishes. This turned out to be a keeper!

1½ cups coarse ground cornmeal
½ cup minced whole green onion
¼ cup Worcestershire sauce
2 tablespoons hot sauce (we use Pico Pica®)
2 tablespoons butter
2 tablespoons honey
1 tablespoon salt
2 cups whole wheat flour
1 cup scalded milk
1 cup hot water
1 tablespoon yeast
¼ cup warm water
4-5 cups white flour

Combine the cornmeal, green onion, Worcestershire sauce, hot sauce, butter, honey, salt, and whole wheat flour in a large mixing bowl. Add the scalded milk and hot water. Mix well. Set aside to cool.

Dissolve the yeast in the warm water and set aside 5-10 minutes.

Combine the dissolved yeast and the cornmeal mixture. Gradually add the white flour until you have a firm dough. Turn onto a floured board and knead until smooth and elastic. Add flour as needed to prevent the dough from sticking. Place in a greased bowl, turning the dough to coat it with oil. Cover and set in a warm place to rise until doubled in bulk, about 1 to 1½ hours.

Punch down the dough and divide into 1¼-pound loaves. Knead briefly to shape and place in greased 4"×6" loaf pans. Let rise until doubled in bulk.

Bake in a preheated 375° oven about 30-35 minutes. Remove from pans, place on cooling rack, and let rest 10 minutes before cutting.

BASIL and SUN-DRIED TOMATO BREAD

Several years ago, we began drying our own tomatoes—now a staple in our kitchen.

2 tablespoons seasoned oil from tomatoes
8 medium shallots, minced
4 large garlic cloves, minced
4½ ounces sun-dried tomatoes, snipped into small pieces
1½ teaspoons salt
1½ cups V8® vegetable juice or tomato juice
3 tablespoons minced fresh basil
   (or 1 tablespoon dried)
1 tablespoon yeast
1 teaspoon sugar
½ cup warm water
2 cups whole wheat flour
2½-3 cups white flour

Heat the seasoned oil in a medium-sized skillet. Add the shallots, garlic, and sun-dried tomatoes, and cook until softened. Transfer to a large mixing bowl and add the salt, V8®, and basil. Set aside to cool.

Dissolve the yeast and sugar in the warm water and set aside 5-10 minutes.

Add the whole wheat flour and dissolved yeast to the mixing bowl and stir to combine. Gradually add the white flour until you have a firm dough. Turn onto a floured board and knead until smooth and elastic. Add flour as needed to prevent the dough from sticking. Place in a greased bowl, turning the dough to coat it with oil. Cover and set in a warm place to rise until doubled in bulk, about 1 to 1½ hours.

Punch down dough and divide into 1¼-pound loaves. Knead briefly to shape and place in greased 4"×6" loaf pans. Let rise until doubled in bulk.

Bake in a preheated 375° oven about 30-35 minutes. Remove from pans, place on cooling rack, and let rest 10 minutes before cutting.

PARSLEY-CHIVE BREAD

A crunchy, fresh herb bread that we frequently serve with pork or fish.

1 cup coarse ground cornmeal
3 tablespoons soft butter
1½ teaspoons salt
1 cup packed fresh parsley leaves, minced
¾ cup chopped fresh chives
1½ cups hot water
2 tablespoons yeast
2 teaspoons sugar
½ cup warm water
2 eggs, beaten
2 cups whole wheat flour
2-3 cups white flour

Place the cornmeal, butter, salt, parsley, and chives in a large mixing bowl. Add the hot water and stir to combine. Set aside to cool.

Dissolve the yeast and sugar in the warm water and set aside 5-10 minutes.

Add the beaten eggs, dissolved yeast, and whole wheat flour to the mixing bowl. Gradually add the white flour until you have a firm dough. Turn onto a floured board and knead until smooth and elastic. Add more flour as needed to prevent the dough from sticking. Place in a greased bowl, turning to coat the dough with oil. Cover and set in a warm place to rise until doubled in bulk, about 1 to 1½ hours.

Punch down and divide into 1¼-pound loaves. Knead briefly to shape and place in greased 4"×6" loaf pans. Let rise until doubled in bulk.

Bake in a preheated 375° oven about 25-30 minutes. Remove from pans, place on cooling rack, and let rest 10 minutes before cutting.

WHOLE WHEAT DILL BREAD

We feel this dill bread is a perfect companion to many fish or lamb entrées. It also makes flavorful toast for seafood spreads and is perfect for a tuna fish sandwich!

3 tablespoons olive oil
½ cup minced onion
2 large garlic cloves, minced
1 teaspoon salt
1 cup cottage cheese
2 tablespoons dried dill weed
1 tablespoon yeast
1 tablespoon sugar
½ cup warm water
2 cups whole wheat flour
2-3 cups white flour

Heat the oil in a medium-sized skillet. Add the onion and garlic, and cook until softened but not brown. Transfer to a large mixing bowl and add the salt, cottage cheese, and dill weed. Set aside to cool.

Dissolve the yeast and sugar in the warm water and set aside 5-10 minutes.

Add the whole wheat flour and dissolved yeast to the mixing bowl. Gradually add the white flour until you have a firm dough. Turn onto a floured board and knead until smooth and elastic. Add flour as needed to prevent the dough from sticking. Place in a greased bowl, turning the dough to coat it with oil. Cover and set in a warm place to rise until doubled in bulk, about 1 to 1½ hours.

Punch down and divide into 1¼-pound loaves. Knead briefly to shape and place in greased 4"×6" loaf pans. Let rise until doubled.

Bake in a preheated 375° oven about 30-35 minutes. Remove from pans, place on cooling rack, and let rest 10 minutes before cutting.

WHOLE WHEAT SEED BREAD

This seed-nut bread fits well in almost any menu and is delightful as breakfast toast. On the evenings we serve this, someone always asks for the recipe—which we are glad to share.

2½ cups warm water
2 tablespoons honey
2 tablespoons yeast
2 tablespoons butter, melted and cooled
⅓ cup molasses
2 teaspoons salt
½ cup wheat germ
¾ cup raw sunflower seeds
¼ cup poppy seeds
¼ cup sesame seeds
⅓ cup sliced almonds
4 cups whole wheat flour
2-2½ cups white flour

Combine the warm water, honey, and yeast in a large mixing bowl. Let set until dissolved, 5-10 minutes.

Add the butter, molasses, salt, wheat germ, sunflower seeds, poppy seeds, sesame seeds, almonds, and whole wheat flour to the yeast mixture. Stir to combine. Gradually add the white flour until you have a firm dough. Turn onto a floured board and knead until smooth and elastic. Add flour as needed to prevent the dough from sticking. Place in a greased bowl, turning the dough to coat it with oil. Cover and set in a warm place to rise until doubled in bulk, about 1 to 1½ hours.

Punch down and divide into 1¼-pound loaves. Knead briefly to shape and place in greased 4" ×6" loaf pans. Let rise until doubled in bulk.

Bake in a preheated 375° oven about 30-35 minutes. Remove from pans, place on cooling rack, and let rest 10 minutes before cutting.

SESAME BREAD

A different bread each evening is one way we plan variety in our menus. This bread, lighter than many of the others, goes well with delicate entrées. It is rather like a crumpet bread when sliced thin and toasted. Try it for breakfast!

2 cups warm water
1 tablespoon honey
2 tablespoons yeast
2 tablespoons sesame oil
½ cup toasted sesame seeds
2 teaspoons salt
4 eggs, beaten
½ cup milk powder
2 cups whole wheat flour
4 cups white flour

Combine the warm water, honey, and yeast in a large bowl. Let set until dissolved, 5-10 minutes.

Add the sesame oil, sesame seeds, salt, beaten eggs, milk powder, and whole wheat flour. Gradually add the white flour until you have a firm dough. Turn onto a floured board and knead until smooth and elastic. Add flour as needed to prevent the dough from sticking. Place in a greased bowl, turning the dough to coat it with oil. Cover and let set in a warm place to rise until doubled in bulk, about 1 to 1½ hours.

Punch down and divide into 1¼-pound loaves. Knead briefly to shape and place in greased 4"×6" loaf pans. Let rise until doubled in bulk.

Bake in a preheated 375° oven about 25-30 minutes. Remove from pans, place on cooling rack, and let rest 10 minutes before cutting.

MILLET BREAD

The millet—often referred to as the "king of grains"—adds an interesting crunch and high nutritional value to an otherwise plain yeast bread.

1 cup oatmeal
1 cup hot milk
3 tablespoons butter, room temperature
1 tablespoon yeast
1 cup warm water
¼ cup honey
2½ teaspoons salt
2 cups whole wheat flour
1½ cups millet
3-3¾ cups white flour

Place the oatmeal in a blender and grind into a flour. Transfer to a large mixing bowl and stir in the hot milk and butter. Cool to room temperature.

Dissolve the yeast in the warm water and honey. Let set 10 minutes.

Add the dissolved yeast, salt, whole wheat flour, and millet to the cooled milk mixture. Mix well. Add 3 cups of the white flour. Stir to combine, adding more white flour if the dough is sticky. Turn onto a floured board and knead until smooth and elastic. Add flour as needed to prevent the dough from sticking. Place in a greased bowl, turning the dough to coat it with oil. Cover and set in a warm place to rise until doubled in bulk, about 1-1½ hours.

Punch down the dough and divide into 1¼-pound loaves. Knead the dough briefly to shape it and place in greased 4"×6" loaf pans. Let rise until doubled in bulk.

Bake in a preheated 375° oven about 30-35 minutes. Remove from pans, place on cooling rack, and let rest 10 minutes before cutting.

HERBED SOURDOUGH BREAD

There are many variables in making a loaf of well-leavened sourdough bread. For those who have not worked with sourdough regularly, it is safest to include some yeast.

¼ cup warm olive oil
2 teaspoons dried thyme
2 teaspoons dried chervil
1 teaspoon freshly ground pepper
¾ cup warm water
1 tablespoon honey
1 tablespoon yeast
3 cups sourdough starter*
2 teaspoons salt
1½ teaspoons baking soda
6 tablespoons milk powder
2 cups whole wheat flour
2½ cups white flour

Combine the warm olive oil, thyme, chervil, and pepper. Set aside for 10 minutes to allow the flavors to meld.

Meanwhile, combine the warm water, yeast, and honey. Let set until bubbly, 5-10 minutes.

Place the sourdough starter in a large mixing bowl. Add the herbed oil, salt, baking soda, milk powder, and dissolved yeast. Mix well. Stir in the whole wheat flour. Gradually add white flour until you have a firm dough. Turn onto a floured board and knead until smooth and elastic. Add flour as needed to prevent dough from sticking. Place in a greased bowl, turning to coat the dough with oil. Cover and let set in a warm place until doubled in bulk, about 1 to 1½ hours.

Punch down and divide into 1¼-pound loaves. Knead briefly to shape and place in greased 4″×6″ loaf pans. Let set to rise until doubled in bulk.

Bake in a preheated 375° oven about 35 minutes. Remove from pans, place on cooling rack, and let rest 10 minutes before cutting.

Variation: Substitute 1 tablespoon of dried rosemary and 2 minced garlic cloves for the thyme, chervil, and pepper.

*Note: If you do not have sourdough starter on hand or can't get some from a friend, you can make your own. The Joy of Cooking is one source for a recipe.

CRACKED WHEAT SOURDOUGH BREAD

The nutty flavor and texture of cracked wheat adds interest to this sourdough bread.

⅔ cup cracked wheat (bulgar)
1½ cups boiling water
1½ cups warm water
½ cup brown sugar
1½ tablespoons yeast
1½ cups sourdough starter
2 teaspoons salt
1 cup milk powder
¼ cup molasses
3 tablespoons vegetable oil
4 cups whole wheat flour
2 cups white flour

One hour prior to dissolving the yeast, place the cracked wheat in a saucepan. Add the boiling water, cover, and let set to soften. Drain in 1 hour and set aside.

Combine the warm water, brown sugar, and yeast. Set aside to dissolve, 5-10 minutes.

Place the sourdough starter in a large mixing bowl. Add the softened cracked wheat, salt, milk powder, molasses, oil, and the dissolved yeast. Mix well. Stir in the 4 cups of whole wheat flour. Gradually add the white flour until you have a firm dough. Turn onto a floured board and knead until smooth and elastic. Add flour as needed to prevent the dough from sticking. Place in a greased bowl, turning the dough to coat it with oil. Cover and set in a warm place to rise until doubled in bulk, about 1 to 1½ hours.

Punch down and divide into 1¼-pound loaves. Knead briefly to shape and place in greased 4″ ×6″ loaf pans. Let rise until doubled in bulk.

Bake in a preheated 375° oven about 30-35 minutes. Remove from pans, place on cooling rack, and let rest 10 minutes before cutting.

SESAME-GARLIC ROLLS

Straight from the oven, these rolls are light and aromatic. The next day they firm up and do not reheat particularly well. Our solution is to cut them in half, brush with butter, and grill them. Then the full flavor of the garlic is released, and they are delightfully crunchy!

2½ cups warm water
2 teaspoons sugar
2 tablespoons yeast
1 teaspoon salt
3 large garlic cloves, minced
⅔ cup freshly grated Parmesan cheese
½ cup wheat germ
1 cup whole wheat flour
3-4 cups white flour
1-2 cups sesame seeds

Using a large mixing bowl, combine the warm water, sugar, and yeast. Set aside until bubbly, 5-10 minutes.

Add the salt, garlic, Parmesan cheese, wheat germ, and whole wheat flour. Add enough white flour to form a soft dough. Turn onto a floured board and knead lightly. Place in a greased bowl, turning the dough to coat it with oil. Cover and set in a warm place to rise until doubled, about 1 hour.

Punch the dough down and break off pieces the size of a golf ball (the dough will be sticky*). Roll balls in sesame seeds and place in greased muffin tins. Let rise until almost doubled.

Bake in a preheated 375° oven about 20-25 minutes. Makes 24-30 rolls.

*If too sticky, knead very briefly. If you lightly coat your hands with butter or oil, the dough will be easier to work with.

CORNMEAL BACON ROLLS

When this recipe was first being developed, a young helper wanted to make the bread for dinner. Well . . . to give you an idea of the results, these tasty rolls are now affectionately known as "Hockey Pucks." Needless to say, we have lightened the recipe so that it doesn't require a degree in bread baking to have them raise properly.

1 cup cornmeal
1½ teaspoon salt
3 tablespoons honey
¼ cup soft butter
1 cup scalded milk
6 ounces bacon
½ cup warm water
2 tablespoons yeast
1 cup whole wheat flour
2 eggs, beaten
2-2½ cups white flour
¼ cup butter, melted

—

Place the cornmeal, salt, honey, and butter in a large mixing bowl. Add the scalded milk. Cut the bacon into ¼" slices and cook until it begins to crispen. Using a slotted spoon, remove from the pan and add to the cornmeal mixture. Let this mixture cool to lukewarm.

Combine the warm water and yeast. Let set until bubbly, 5-10 minutes.

Add the whole wheat flour, beaten eggs, and dissolved yeast to the cooled cornmeal mixture. Mix well. Gradually add enough white flour until you have a soft dough. Turn onto a floured board and knead until smooth. Place in a greased bowl, turning the dough to coat it with oil. Cover and set in a warm place to rise until doubled in bulk.

Punch the dough down and pinch off pieces the size of a golf ball. Shape into buns, roll in the melted butter, and place on a baking sheet or in muffin tins. Let rise 30 minutes.

Bake in a preheated 375° oven about 20 minutes. Makes 24-30 buns or muffins.

PEPPER CHEESE MUFFINS

These pepper muffins are a quick so-lution when you do not have time to bake a yeast bread.

2 cups flour
1 tablespoon baking powder
½ teaspoon salt
1½-2 teaspoons freshly ground pepper
1 tablespoon sugar
1 cup grated Cheddar cheese, preferably sharp
1 cup buttermilk
1 egg, beaten
⅓ cup butter, melted

Combine the flour, baking powder, salt, pepper, sugar, and cheese. Mix the buttermilk, beaten egg, and melted butter. Add to the dry ingredients. Stir just long enough to combine. Divide among 12 greased muffin tins and bake in a preheated 400° oven about 20-25 minutes.

HERB BISCUITS

A rich, melt-in-your-mouth biscuit! When you run short on time, it is another quick solution for a dinner bread.

1¾ cups flour
1 tablespoon baking powder
1 tablespoon sugar
½ teaspoon salt
2 tablespoons minced fresh parsley
1 tablespoon chopped fresh chives
Pinch cayenne pepper
½ cup cold butter, cut in chunks
½ cup plus 2 tablespoons whipping cream
1 egg, beaten

Combine the flour, baking powder, sugar, salt, parsley, chives, and cayenne. Cut in the butter. Combine the whipping cream and egg. Stir into the dry ingredients until the dough begins to hold together. Turn onto a floured board and knead with two swift strokes to smooth out the dough. Using a rolling pin or your hands, flatten the dough to ½" thick. Cut with a 3" round biscuit cutter. Place on an ungreased baking sheet.

Bake in a preheated 425° oven about 15 minutes or until lightly browned. Makes 10 biscuits.

GRANDMA'S BREAD

Jeanne Moore's mother, "Grandma Maes," was the originator of Grandma's Bread. She would bake two or three batches of bread during a stay at the Inn. It was not a regular menu item then, as it is now, and only those "in the know" had access to the wonderfully delicious bread. For many of our guests, having Grandma's Bread for breakfast is a part of the ritual of coming to the Inn. Be aware of the proportions in this recipe!

Combine in a large bowl:
2 cups wheat germ
1½ cups cornmeal
⅓ cup carob powder
2 cups soy flour
14 cups whole wheat flour
7 teaspoons salt
2 cups sunflower seeds
2 cups milk powder
½ cup brewers yeast powder
2 cups millet
4 cups white flour

Cook oats:
Cook ½ cup regular oats in 1½ cups water 10 minutes, or cover with water and cook in microwave 1 minute.

Combine and set aside:
3 tablespoons yeast
½ cup lukewarm water
1 teaspoon honey

Combine in a large bowl:
9 cups hot water
1½ cups honey
1½ cups oil
2 cups carrot puree

Combine *all* ingredients in the large bowl. Add more white flour until the dough is a consistency that can be kneaded. Turn onto a floured board and knead. (Sometimes it is easiest to knead it half at a time.) Place in an oiled bowl. Cover and let rise in a warm place 1 to 1½ hours.

Punch down and let rise again. Divide into 1¼-pound loaves. Knead and place in oiled 1-pound coffee cans. While the oven is preheating, let the bread rise to the third ring in the can.

Bake in a 350° oven about 40-50 minutes, rotating the loaves if necessary. Makes 16-18 loaves. (It freezes well!)

Note: The original recipe had several additional ingredients such as dolomite, rice polish, and graham flour, some of which cannot be easily found. After having the recipe evaluated by a nutritionist, it was suggested some substitutions could be made without affecting the overall nutritional value, thus shortening the list of necessary ingredients. We have added grated carrot for moisture and the millet for additional texture.

Desserts

Ah, dessert. The main course dishes, most of them cleaned to the last morsel, have been cleared from the table. Appetites have been sated and most guests are beginning to feel the effects of a long day's exercise and the evening's full repast. The hour is growing late, and here and there a yawn has been stifled.

To truly entice—after so many hearty courses and perhaps too many glasses of wine—a dessert must be, well, flamboyant. Or possibly a bit mysterious. Or maybe even flirtatious. At the Steamboat Inn, dessert may be all these things—and more.

If the Fisherman's Dinner were a play—and with its cast of characters and unique setting, it has all the necessary elements—then dessert must be the climactic scene. The players have all been introduced, and the evening has seen its share of character development. Preceding courses have laid the foundation and established the plot line. Now dessert must pull all these diverse elements together, provide a satisfying denouement, and leave the guests wishing for just a little more. It's a big order.

But, somehow, Pat and Sharon have always been up to the challenge. Some of their desserts are light and tantalizing, zesty without being overbearing. Others may be sinfully rich. After all, the Fisherman's Dinner is a celebration of the river. What celebration would be complete without some fireworks to bring down the house in the final act?

Dessert at the Steamboat Inn complements the meal and provides its finishing touch. If the entrée has been hearty—perhaps beef tenderloin or leg of lamb—then Sharon and Pat will balance it with a light dessert. A sorbet will often provide welcome relief for dinner guests who thought they couldn't possibly eat another bite. But most nights, Pat and Sharon don't hold back; they let the guests beware when dessert rolls around. Most choose to take the plunge—the temptation is simply too great!

After the last delicious crumb has been consumed and the curtain has been drawn on dessert, the guests excuse themselves and make their exits. Their satisfied voices can be heard exclaiming over dinner as they wander down the flagstone paths to their cabins. Then the purling of the river is the only sound that remains, lulling guests and hosts alike to sleep.

ALMOND CAKE with FRESH FRUIT

This rich almond cake is a perfect companion to fresh strawberries, raspberries, or sliced peaches. This versatile cake freezes well and is, therefore, easy to keep on hand.

3 cups sifted cake flour
¼ teaspoon salt
4½ teaspoons baking powder
6 tablespoons butter
6 tablespoons shortening
2 cups sugar
¾ teaspoon vanilla extract
½ teaspoon almond extract
1 cup plus 2 tablespoons milk
9 egg whites
2 cups whipping cream
2 teaspoons berry liqueur or peach schnapps
    (optional)
2 cups fresh fruit, sweetened if necessary

Grease and flour three 9" cake pans and set aside.
    Sift the flour, salt, and baking powder.
    Thoroughly cream the butter and shortening. Gradually add 1½ cups sugar. Add the vanilla and almond extracts. Alternately, add the sifted dry ingredients and the milk to the creamed mixture.

Beat the egg whites until foamy. Gradually add 6 tablespoons of the sugar and continue to beat until stiff peaks form. Stir ¼ of the whites into the batter to lighten it. Gently fold in the remaining whites and pour into the greased cake pans. Bake in a preheated 350° oven for about 20-30 minutes, until a toothpick inserted in the center comes out clean. Remove from the oven and the pans. Set on a baking rack to cool.

Just before serving, whip the cream with the remaining 2 tablespoons sugar and the liqueur. Using 2 of the cake layers, place 1 on a serving plate. Cover with a layer of sweetened cream and ⅔ of the fruit. Cover with the second layer and frost the outside with the remaining cream. Garnish the top with the remaining fruit. Freeze the remaining cake layer. Serves 12-16.

CITRUS GÂTEAU with BAVARIAN CREAM

When we were in France, we observed a pastry demonstration given by the head pastry chef at Maxim's. The loveliest dessert was an Orange Chanticleer. We were given the recipe but were unsuccessful with the English conversions of the ingredients. Although the cake and filling are different, we were able to replicate the appearance. It is a stunning dessert for very special occasions.

1 9" buttered cake pan
1 9" layer Citrus Gâteau (recipe follows)
Candied Orange Slices (recipe follows)
Bavarian Cream (recipe follows)

Reserving the syrup, place the orange slices on paper towels to absorb excess moisture

Cut the cake into three layers. Set one aside for another use. Brush the remaining two layers with some of the reserved orange syrup.

To assemble: Arrange the orange slices in an interesting pattern on the bottom and along the side of the buttered cake pan. (Use half slices to fill in and finish off the outer edge.) Spread ⅓ of the Bavarian cream in the bottom of the pan to cover the orange slices. Top with a cake layer and gently press down to fill the cream in among the orange slices. Top with the remaining ⅔ Bavarian cream. Add the remaining cake layer and gently press down again to distribute the cream along the edges of the cake layer and the pan. Cover and refrigerate 4-5 hours or overnight. The assembled cake will hold for 2-3 days under refrigeration. Serves 10-12.

To unmold: Place a plate on top of the cake pan and invert the pan. Run a warmed towel along the sides and the bottom of the pan to loosen the filling. Turn the cake pan, right side up, and gently tap the entire outside edge to loosen the filling—you should see the cake releasing from the sides of the pan. Invert the cake onto the serving platter. Give the bottom of the pan a couple of taps and the cake should release completely.

◆

CITRUS GÂTEAU

1¼ cups sifted cake flour
1¼ teaspoons baking powder
⅛ teaspoon salt
⅓ cup butter, room temperature
2 teaspoons orange zest
1 teaspoon lemon zest
¾ cup sugar
2 egg yolks
1½ teaspoons lemon juice
1½ teaspoons orange liqueur
6 tablespoons milk
3 egg whites

Grease and flour one 9" cake pan. Set aside. Sift the flour, baking powder, and salt. Set aside.

Cream the butter and orange and lemon zests. Gradually add the sugar. Add the egg yolks one at a time, making sure the first is incorporated before adding the next. Mix in the lemon juice and orange liqueur. Alternately add the sifted flour and the milk to the batter.

Beat the egg whites until stiff but not dry. Stir ¼ of the whites into the batter to lighten it. Gently fold in the remaining whites. Pour into the prepared cake pan.

Bake in a preheated 375° oven for about 20-25 minutes, until a toothpick inserted in the center comes out clean. Remove from the oven. Remove cake from the pan and set on a rack to cool.

CANDIED ORANGE SLICES

2 whole medium oranges
½ cup sugar
½ cup water
1½ teaspoons orange liqueur

Using a very sharp knife, thinly slice the oranges. Place the sugar and water in a medium-size saucepan and stir over medium heat until the sugar dissolves. Add the orange slices and simmer gently 10 minutes. Remove from the heat, add the liqueur and set aside to cool. These will hold for quite some time if left in the syrup, covered tightly, and refrigerated.

BAVARIAN CREAM

1 cup milk
Zest of two oranges
¼ cup sugar
5 egg yolks
1 package gelatin
Juice of two oranges
½ cup whipping cream
1 tablespoon powdered sugar

Combine the milk, zest, and ¼ cup of the sugar in a saucepan and gently heat. Remove from the heat and strain, discarding the zest. Beat the egg yolks with the remaining sugar. With the mixer running, slowly add the heated milk. Return this mixture to the saucepan and heat, stirring constantly, until thickened. Do not boil. The mixture should heavily coat a spoon. Remove from the heat. Soften the gelatin in two tablespoons of the orange juice, then warm it to dissolve. Add the dissolved gelatin to the custard and stir until well incorporated. Place the custard in a bowl set in a pan of ice water and stir until it cools and thickens. Remove from the ice water. Whip the cream with the powdered sugar. Fold the whipped cream and orange juice into the thickened custard. Assemble the gâteau.

WALNUT CAKE with WALNUT PRALINE MOUSSE

The Walnut Cake is light and airy, an ideal mate for the rich mousse filling.

1¾ cups sifted flour
1 tablespoon baking powder
¼ teaspoon salt
½ cup butter, room temperature
1¼ cups sugar
½ teaspoon vanilla extract
Scant ¼ teaspoon walnut extract
¾ cup milk
6 egg whites
½ cup ground walnuts
1 recipe Walnut Praline Mousse (recipe
    follows)
2½ cups whipping cream
⅓ cup Praline (recipe follows)

Grease and flour two 9" cake pans. Set aside. Sift the flour, baking powder, and salt. Set aside.

Cream the butter and 1 cup of the sugar. Add the vanilla and walnut extracts. Alternately add the sifted flour and the milk to the creamed butter mixture.

Beat the egg whites until foamy. Gradually add the remaining ¼ cup sugar and continue to beat until stiff. Stir ¼ of the whites and the walnuts into the batter to lighten it. Gently fold in the remaining egg whites. Pour into the two prepared cake pans.

Bake in a preheated 350° oven for about 20-25 minutes until a toothpick inserted in the center comes out clean. Remove from the oven. Remove the cake from the pans and set on a rack to cool.

To assemble: Whip the cream and fold in the ⅓ cup praline. Place one cake layer on a serving platter. Top with the walnut praline mousse. Cover the mousse with the remaining cake layer and frost the sides and top with the whipped cream. Serves 10-12.

WALNUT PRALINE MOUSSE

3 tablespoons water
1 package gelatin
3 egg yolks
¼ cup milk
2 tablespoons rum or brandy
2 drops walnut extract
½ cup Praline (recipe follows)
2 egg whites, room temperature
¾ cup whipping cream

Sprinkle the gelatin over the water and let set a few minutes to soften. Warm the gelatin gently to dissolve. Thoroughly combine the egg yolks, milk, rum, and walnut extract. Add the ground praline and mix well. Add the dissolved gelatin and stir until well combined. Set aside.

Whip the egg whites until soft peaks form.

Whip the cream until soft peaks form.

Place the egg yolk-gelatin mixture in a medium-size mixing bowl. Set the mixing bowl in a pan of ice water. Stir until the mixture starts to thicken. Remove the bowl from the ice water before the mixture starts to set. (The egg whites, whipped cream, and egg yolk-gelatin mixture should all be the same consistency.) Gently fold egg whites and whipped cream into the egg yolk-gelatin mixture. Refrigerate 1-2 hours.

PRALINE

½ cup plus 3 tablespoons sugar
½ cup toasted walnut halves

Line a baking sheet with aluminum foil; set aside. Place the sugar in a heavy skillet over medium heat. Stir until the sugar starts to dissolve. Continue cooking, without stirring, until the sugar is dark brown. Add the toasted walnuts and stir to coat. Turn out onto foil-lined baking sheet and let set to cool. When cool, grind. Makes about ¾ cup ground praline.

FILBERT ANGEL FOOD CAKE

The toasted filberts and brown sugar add interest and a wonderful flavor.

2 cups sifted brown sugar
1¼ cups cake flour
1 teaspoon baking powder
½ teaspoon salt
½ teaspoon instant espresso powder
1½ cups egg whites (about 12 whites),
    room temperature
1½ teaspoons cream of tartar
3 tablespoons filbert liqueur
½ cup ground toasted filberts
Filbert Icing (recipe follows)

Sift together 1 cup of the brown sugar, the cake flour, baking powder, salt, and espresso powder.

Beat the egg whites with the cream of tartar until foamy. Gradually beat in the remaining sifted brown sugar and continue to beat until stiff. Fold in 1 teaspoon filbert liqueur, then the sifted dry ingredients and the ground filberts. Pour into an ungreased tube pan—one with a removable rim. Run the blade of a spatula through the dough to remove any air bubbles.

Bake in a preheated 350° oven for about 45 minutes. Remove from the oven and cool in the pan. Remove from the pan and slice into 3 layers. Sprinkle the layers with the remaining filbert liqueur. Fill and ice. Serves 12-14.

FILBERT ICING

¼ cup butter
½ cup brown sugar
1 tablespoon cornstarch
2 tablespoons filbert liqueur
4 egg yolks
¾ cup ground toasted filberts
1½ cups whipping cream

Melt the butter in a small-size saucepan. Add the brown sugar, cornstarch, filbert liqueur, and egg yolks. Mix well. Cook, stirring constantly, until thickened. Add the ground nuts. Set aside to cool.

Whip the cream and fold in the cooled egg yolk mixture. Makes enough for one 3-layer cake.

WALNUT ROULADE with CHOCOLATE and FRESH STRAWBERRIES

A superb late spring dessert combining fresh strawberries, chocolate, and walnuts.

¾ cup cake flour
1 teaspoon baking powder
¼ teaspoon salt
4 egg yolks
¾ cup sugar
½ teaspoon vanilla extract
¼ teaspoon walnut extract
4 egg whites
Pinch of cream of tartar
¾ cup finely ground walnuts
6 ounces semisweet chocolate
3 tablespoons butter
1 pint strawberries
1 tablespoon berry or orange liqueur
1 cup whipping cream
2 tablespoons sugar

Line a jelly roll pan with buttered parchment. Set aside.

Sift the flour, baking powder, and salt.

Beat the egg yolks with ¼ cup sugar until thick. Add the vanilla and ⅛ teaspoon walnut extracts. Add the sifted dry ingredients and the ground walnuts. (The mixture will be thick.)

Beat the egg whites with the cream of tartar until foamy. Gradually add the remaining ½ cup sugar and continue to beat until stiff. Stir ¼ of the beaten whites into the batter to lighten it. Gently fold in the remaining whites and spread in the jelly roll pan. Bake in a preheated 375° oven for about 12-15 minutes, rotating the pan halfway through cooking.

While the cake is baking, lay out a kitchen towel (not terry cloth) and dust with powdered sugar. When the cake is done, remove from the oven and invert the pan onto the towel. Remove the pan and peel back the parchment. Starting at the short end, roll up the cake in the towel. Set aside on a rack to cool.

Combine the chocolate and butter in the top part of a double boiler. Melt over simmering water.

Reserve 3 whole berries for garnish and slice the remainder. Sweeten with powdered sugar, if necessary, and add the liqueur.

Whip the cream with the 2 tablespoons sugar and remaining ⅛ teaspoon walnut extract until soft peaks form.

Unroll the cake and remove from the towel. Place on a work surface. Trim the edges if necessary. Spread a layer of the melted chocolate on the entire exposed surface of the cake. Cover with a layer of the sliced strawberries. Spread all but ¼ cup of the whipped cream over the berries. Carefully roll up and transfer to a serving platter. Using the remaining chocolate, spread a 3″ band of chocolate along the top of the roll. Refrigerate 10 minutes to set the chocolate. Pipe the reserved ¼ cup whipping cream along the chocolate strip and garnish with the reserved whole berries. This may be assembled 2-3 hours prior to serving and cuts best with a serrated knife. Serves 8-10.

A winter variation: **Substitute** ground toasted filberts for the walnuts and replace the walnut extract with filbert liqueur. Use the Filling (recipe following) as a substitution for the chocolate and fresh strawberry filling.

Filling:
2 cups cranberries, fresh or frozen
2 cups frozen strawberries, partially thawed
2 tablespoons filbert liqueur
2 tablespoons cornstarch

Cook the cranberries and the strawberries in a small saucepan until the cranberries start to pop. Transfer to a food processor or blender and puree. Return to the saucepan along with the filbert liqueur and cornstarch. Cook until thickened and set aside to cool. Use in place of the chocolate and fresh strawberries in the roulade.

Note: Do not be alarmed at the mushy state of the frozen strawberries as they thaw. It will not have any effect on the end product.

CHOCOLATE FILBERT PÂTÉ

A dense chocolate dessert — the answer to your wildest chocolate fantasy!

12 ounces semisweet chocolate
2 tablespoons butter
2 tablespoons strong coffee
3 tablespoons filbert liqueur
1 tablespoon vanilla extract
3 egg yolks
½ cup whipping cream
2 tablespoons sugar
¼ cup *coarsely* chopped filberts
White Chocolate Sauce (optional) (page 120)

Mix a couple of drops of oil into ¼ cup water and lightly brush a 4″×6″ loaf pan (or 3-cup mold of your choice).

Melt the chocolate, butter, and coffee in the top of a double boiler over simmering water. Remove from the heat and add the liqueur and vanilla. Beat in the egg yolks one at a time, making sure the first is incorporated before adding the next. Cool to room temperature.

Whip the cream with the 2 tablespoons sugar until soft peaks form.

Stir ½ of the whipped cream into the chocolate mixture. Gently fold in the remaining cream and coarsely chopped filberts. Place in a lightly greased mold and refrigerate 2-3 hours until set. Slice and serve. Serves 8-10.

To unmold: Wrap a warmed kitchen towel around the base of the mold and invert onto a serving platter. With the warmth of the towel, the pâté should slide right out.

Note: We sometimes serve this in a pool of white chocolate sauce.

CHOCOLATE CRÊPE GÂTEAU

This is Dan Callaghan's favorite Steamboat Inn dessert—delicate chocolate crêpes filled with a smooth chocolate mousse, then frozen. The final touch is a spoonful of white chocolate sauce and a drop of raspberry puree.

2 recipes Chocolate Mousse (page 121)
White Chocolate Sauce (recipe follows)
Raspberry Puree (page 123)
1½ cups milk
1 cup flour
⅓ cup sugar
3 eggs
3 tablespoons unsweetened cocoa powder
1½ teaspoons vanilla extract
1½ tablespoons butter, melted and cooled to room temperature

Place the milk, flour, sugar, eggs, cocoa, and vanilla in a blender. Blend on high until combined—do not overblend. Pour into a bowl and stir in the melted butter. Let the batter rest one hour.

Brush a 10″ skillet with butter. Heat. Using a ¼ cup measure, spoon the batter into the skillet, tilting the pan to distribute the batter to the edges. Cook one minute, turn over, and cook an additional 30 seconds. Remove from the pan and place on waxed paper. Continue with the remaining batter, buttering the pan as needed. Makes 12-16 crêpes.*

When the crêpes are cool, lay one on a serving plate. Cover with a layer of chocolate mousse—spreading it all the way to the outer edge of the crêpe and top with another crêpe. Continue in this manner until you have used 6 crêpes and have 5 layers of chocolate—ending up with a crêpe on top. Cover and freeze. Makes two 6-layer gâteaus, serving 6 people each.

Thirty-five minutes prior to serving, remove the gâteau from the freezer and place in your refrigerator for 30 minutes. Pull from the refrigerator and let set 5 minutes, then cut into 6 pieces each. Place on individual serving dishes and spoon warm White Chocolate Sauce over the gâteau (about 2 tablespoons). Top with a small dollop of Raspberry Puree and serve.

If you have more crêpes than you need, they freeze well and defrost quickly when needed.

WHITE CHOCOLATE SAUCE

½ pound (8 ounces) high quality white chocolate
1 cup heavy cream
¼ cup brandy, rum, or a nut liqueur of your choice

Thinly shave the white chocolate or process in a food processor until finely ground.

Heat the heavy cream and liqueur in a pan over medium heat. Cook until the cream starts to thicken. Remove from the heat and add the white chocolate, stirring until it is well combined. If it is lumpy, blend to smooth it out. The sauce can be done ahead and reheated before serving. The sauce stores well under refrigeration as the liqueur helps to preserve the cream.

CHOCOLATE MOUSSE TART

A velvety-smooth filling encased in a nutty crust—oh, so satisfying!

1 10″ tart pan with a removable bottom
1 recipe Chocolate Nut Crust (recipe follows)
1 tablespoon cold coffee
1 teaspoon instant coffee powder
1 teaspoon vanilla extract
1 teaspoon brandy, rum, or any nut liqueur
3 egg yolks, room temperature
3 ounces unsweetened chocolate
3 ounces semisweet chocolate
12 tablespoons sugar
6 tablespoons water
3 egg whites, room temperature
Pinch of cream of tartar
⅓ cup whipping cream

Prepare and bake the crust. Set aside to cool.

Combine the coffee, instant coffee, vanilla, brandy, and egg yolks. Set aside.

Chunk up the chocolate and place in the bowl of a food processor. Process until finely ground.

Combine 6 tablespoons sugar and the water in a small saucepan and heat on high, without stirring, until the sugar has dissolved and the mixture just starts to boil. Turn on the food processor and very carefully pour the hot sugar syrup through the feed tube. Process until combined. Scrape down the sides of the work bowl and let set 2 minutes to cool a bit. Then add the coffee-egg yolk mixture and process until smooth. Transfer to a mixing bowl.

Beat the egg whites and cream of tartar until foamy. Gradually add the remaining 6 tablespoons sugar and continue to beat until stiff, shiny peaks form. Stir ¼ of the whites into the chocolate-egg yolk mixture to lighten it. Gently fold in the remaining whites.

Whip the cream until soft peaks form and gently fold into the chocolate. Pour into the prepared crust and chill 4-5 hours or overnight. Serves 10.

CHOCOLATE NUT CRUST

4 ounces semisweet chocolate, finely ground
⅓ cup finely ground walnuts
2 cups finely ground vanilla wafers
6 tablespoons butter, melted

Combine the chocolate, nuts, and ground wafers. Stir in the melted butter until well combined. Press onto the sides and bottom of a lightly buttered 10″ tart pan. Chill 10 minutes. Bake in a preheated 375° oven about 10 minutes. Remove and set on a rack to cool.

PEAR TART

Fresh pear, streusel, and almond pastry—a wonderful combination!

1 10" tart pan with a removable bottom
½ recipe Rich Almond Pastry (recipe
   follows), baked 10 minutes
¾ cup sour cream
½ cup sugar
1 egg
7 tablespoons flour
2 teaspoons pear brandy
Pinch of salt
4 cups thinly sliced fresh pears
3 tablespoons white sugar
3 tablespoons brown sugar
½ teaspoon freshly ground nutmeg
½ cup chopped walnuts
4 tablespoons butter, cut in chunks

Combine the sour cream, sugar, egg, 3 tablespoons flour, pear brandy, and salt.

Arrange the pear slices in the almond crust. Pour the sour cream mixture over the fruit. Place in a preheated 450° oven and bake about 10 minutes. Reduce the heat to 350° and continue baking for 35 minutes.

Meanwhile, combine the remaining 4 tablespoons flour, the white and brown sugars, nutmeg, and walnuts. Cut in the butter. Remove the tart from the oven and top with the streusel. Return to the oven and continue to cook until nicely browned, about 15 minutes. Serve warm or at room temperature. Serves 8-10.

RICH ALMOND PASTRY

1 cup plus 6 tablespoons flour
¾ cup finely ground almonds
6 tablespoons sugar
¼ teaspoon salt
11 tablespoons unsalted butter, cut in chunks
¼ teaspoon vanilla extract
¼ teaspoon almond extract
2 egg yolks

Combine the flour, nuts, sugar, and salt. Cut in the butter. Stir together the extracts and egg yolks. Add to the flour and butter mixture, working just long enough to bind the ingredients. Turn onto a floured board and knead two swift strokes to form into a ball.

Divide in two and flatten each piece into a round disk. Wrap each piece in saran and chill 20 minutes. Roll the chilled pastry out between two sheets of floured saran wrap. At this stage the dough is very delicate and can be difficult to transfer to the tart pan. Do not despair—it will be well worth the extra effort! Just press it into place and trim the edges by running your thumb along the rim of the tart pan. Chill 30 minutes.

Remove from the refrigerator and line the pan with foil and weight down with beans or rice. Bake for 15 minutes in a preheated 400° oven. Remove the foil and weights and return to the oven and bake an additional 5 minutes, until nicely browned. Makes enough for 2 10" tarts.

CREAM CHEESE MOUSSE with RASPBERRY and BRANDY SAUCES

This is a great choice when you are looking for an elegant, though not overly rich, dessert.

1 envelope gelatin
1 tablespoon brandy
½ cup cold water
8 ounces cream cheese, room temperature
6 tablespoons sugar
2 egg yolks, room temperature
¼ cup light cream (half and half)
3 tablespoons lemon juice
Zest of 1 medium lemon
2 egg whites, room temperature
1 cup whipping cream
Raspberry Puree (recipe follows)
Brandy Sauce (recipe follows)

Prepare 8 half-cup molds by lightly brushing them with water that has had a small amount of oil mixed into it. Set aside.

Sprinkle the gelatin over the brandy and water and let set until softened. Gently warm the mixture until the gelatin has dissolved.

Beat the cream cheese and gradually add the sugar. Scrape down the sides of the mixing bowl to make sure all the sugar has been incorporated. Add the egg yolks one at a time, making sure the first has been fully incorporated before adding the next. Add the light cream, lemon juice, and zest. Mix well. Add the dissolved gelatin and mix well to thoroughly combine. Transfer to a medium-size mixing bowl and set aside.

Beat the egg whites until soft peaks form.

Beat the whipping cream until soft peaks form.

Place the bowl of cream cheese mixture in a pan of ice water. Stir constantly until the mixture starts to thicken—but not set. (For best results the cream cheese mixture, egg whites, and whipped cream should all be the same consistency.) Fold the egg whites into the cream cheese. Then fold in the whipped cream carefully to avoid creating any lumps. Fill the prepared molds with the mousse and refrigerate until set, about 4 hours.

To unmold: Loosen the edges with a spatula, dip the forms in warm water, wipe them dry, and invert onto a chilled baking sheet. The mousse should slip out of the mold. Continue with the remaining molds.

Lay out 8 chilled dessert plates. Place 2 tablespoons Raspberry Puree on each plate. Using a cake spatula, transfer a mousse to each dessert plate, setting it on the Raspberry Puree. Top each mousse with 2 tablespoons Brandy Sauce. Serve immediately. Serves eight.

◆

RASPBERRY PUREE

12 ounces unsweetened frozen raspberries
⅓ cup sugar (more or less to taste)
1 tablespoon orange liqueur (optional)

Puree and strain the raspberries. Add the sugar and orange liqueur (optional) to the raspberries. Mix well. Makes 1-1¼ cups puree.

◆

BRANDY SAUCE

¾ cup sugar
1 tablespoon cornstarch
1 cup water
3 egg yolks, lightly beaten
1 tablespoon brandy

Combine the sugar and cornstarch in a small saucepan. Gradually stir in the water. Cook over medium heat until clear and thickened. Add a small amount to the egg yolks to warm them, then stir the warmed yolks into the saucepan. Cook, stirring constantly, 2 minutes. Remove from the heat and stir in the brandy. Set aside to cool. Makes 1½ cups sauce.

LEMON BLUEBERRY CRÊPES

A perfect summer dessert composed of light lemon crêpes, lemon curd, and luscious fresh blueberries with a dash of whipped cream.

1½ cups milk
1 cup sifted flour
4 eggs
2 tablespoons sugar
⅛ teaspoon freshly grated nutmeg
2 tablespoons orange liqueur
1 teaspoon lemon zest
¼ cup butter, melted and cooled to room
   temperature
Lemon Curd (recipe follows)
1½ cups whipping cream
2 cups blueberries

Combine the milk, flour, eggs, sugar, nutmeg, orange liqueur and lemon zest in a blender. Blend at high speed until mixed, scraping down the sides of the blender to make sure all the ingredients are incorporated. Pour into a mixing bowl and add the melted butter. Stir to blend and let rest at least 30 minutes.

Brush a 10″ skillet with butter. Heat. Add ¼ cup crêpe batter, tilting the pan to distribute the batter to the edges. Cook 1 minute, flip over and cook an additional 30 seconds. Remove from the pan and place on waxed paper. Continue with the remaining batter, buttering the pan as needed. Set aside to cool. Makes 12-14 crêpes.

To assemble: Lay 8-10 crêpes out on a work surface and coat each with a thin layer of lemon curd. Whip the cream and fold in the remaining curd and all but a few of the blueberries. Lay ½ to ¾ cup filling in the middle of each crêpe. Fold the crêpe in half and press to distribute the filling, then fold again into a wedge shape and place on an individual serving plate. Garnish with the reserved berries. Serves 8-10.

LEMON CURD

¾ cup sugar
1 tablespoon cornstarch
Zest of 1 large lemon
Juice of 2 small lemons (about ½ cup)
4 egg yolks
6 tablespoons butter, melted

Mix together the sugar and cornstarch. Stir in the zest, lemon juice, and egg yolks. Add the melted butter and mix well. Transfer to a small, non-corrosive saucepan and cook, stirring constantly, until thickened. Do not let the mixture boil. Remove from the heat and transfer to a mixing bowl. Cover with a piece of wax paper and set aside to cool. Makes 1-1¼ cups lemon curd.

RHUBARB UPSIDE-DOWN CAKE

Fresh rhubarb complemented by a touch of sherry and topped with a light cake.

3 tablespoons butter, melted
½ cup brown sugar
2 cups ½" sliced rhubarb
3-4 tablespoons dry sherry
⅔ cup flour
1 teaspoon baking powder
⅛ teaspoon salt
2 egg yolks, room temperature
1 teaspoon lemon juice
⅔ cup sugar
½ teaspoon vanilla extract
3 tablespoons hot water
2 egg whites, room temperature
Whipped cream for garnish (optional)

Place the melted butter in a 10" pie plate. Sprinkle the brown sugar evenly over the bottom of the pie pan. Add the rhubarb in an even layer and sprinkle with the sherry.

Sift the flour, baking powder, and salt.

Beat the egg yolks and lemon juice until thickened. Gradually add the sugar and the vanilla. Beat until thick and fluffy. Slowly add the hot water, one tablespoon at a time. Stir in the sifted dry ingredients.

Beat the egg whites until stiff but not dry. Fold ¼ of the whites into the batter to lighten it. Gently fold in the remaining whites. Pour the cake batter over the rhubarb, covering it completely. Bake in a preheated 325° oven about 40-45 minutes. Remove from the oven and let stand 10 minutes. Loosen the edges and invert onto a plate. Serve warm. Garnish with whipped cream, if desired. Serves 6-8.

BLUEBERRY SHORTCAKE

The slightly sweet orange biscuit is a perfect partner for the blueberries.

1¾ cups flour
1 tablespoon baking powder
1 tablespoon sugar
½ teaspoon salt
1 tablespoon orange zest
½ cup cold butter, cut in chunks
1 egg
½ cup whipping cream
2 tablespoons orange liqueur
1 quart blueberries, fresh or frozen
¼ cup sugar
2 tablespoons light corn syrup
Zest of 1 large orange
½ teaspoon freshly grated nutmeg

Sift the flour, baking powder, sugar, and salt. Stir in the tablespoon of orange zest. Cut in the butter until the mixture resembles coarse meal. Combine the egg, cream, and orange liqueur and add to the flour mixture. Stir just until the mixture starts to hold together. Turn onto a floured board and knead two swift strokes to bind the dough. Using a rolling pin or your hands, flatten to ½" thick. Cut with a 3" biscuit cutter and place on an ungreased baking sheet. Bake in a preheated 425° oven about 15-20 minutes until the tops start to brown. Makes 10 biscuits.

While the biscuits are baking, crush half of the blueberries in a medium-size saucepan. Add the remaining berries, sugar, corn syrup, orange zest, and nutmeg. Cook until thickened.

Place half of a biscuit in a serving dish and cover with warm blueberries. Top with the remaining half biscuit and more berries. Serve immediately. Serves 10.

APPLE-BLACKBERRY CRISP

This recipe is at its very best in early summer when the wild blackberries are in season. A good "second best" can be accomplished with boysenberries or marionberries.

1 pound apples, peeled, cored, and sliced
1 pound wild blackberries
½ cup sugar
3 teaspoons vanilla extract
1½ teaspoons cinnamon
1 teaspoon freshly ground nutmeg
½ cup coarsely chopped walnuts
¾ cup flour
¾ cup packed dark brown sugar
¼ cup rolled oats
¼ teaspoon salt
½ cup cold butter, cut in chunks

Butter a 9″×9″ baking pan. Set aside. Combine the sliced apples, berries, sugar, 1 teaspoon vanilla, ½ teaspoon cinnamon, and ½ teaspoon nutmeg. Spoon into the buttered baking pan.

Combine the walnuts, flour, brown sugar, oats, salt, and the remaining 2 teaspoons vanilla, 1 teaspoon cinnamon, and ½ teaspoon nutmeg. Cut in the butter. Spread over the apples. Bake in a preheated 350° oven about 45-60 minutes until the top is crisp and brown. Serves 6-8.

FRESH PEACHES with PRALINE and RASPBERRY PUREE

A perfect ending to a light meal. The succulent flavor of fresh peaches is intensified by the Raspberry Puree. The essence of summer!

6 cups peach slices
1¼ cups Raspberry Puree (page 123)
2 egg yolks
1 teaspoon vanilla extract
1 cup sifted powdered sugar
1 cup whipping cream, whipped
7 tablespoons ground Praline (page 116)

Combine the peaches and the Raspberry Puree, tossing well to coat the peaches. Set aside.

Combine the egg yolks and vanilla. Add the powdered sugar, mixing until well blended. Fold in the whipped cream and 6 tablespoons ground Praline.

Divide the peaches among 6 serving dishes and top with the whipped cream mixture. Garnish with the remaining tablespoon of ground Praline. Serves 6.

PEAR-CRANBERRY SORBET

This unique pear-cranberry combination is intriguing to our guests. It is well complemented by a crisp, not-too-sweet cookie.

¾ pound ripe pears, pared and sliced
½ pound whole cranberries, fresh or frozen
1 cup water
1 cup sugar

Combine all the ingredients in a medium-size saucepan and cook until the cranberries have popped and the pears are soft. Transfer to a blender or food processor and process until smooth. Set aside to cool.

When cool, churn in an ice cream maker, following the manufacturer's instructions. When churned, transfer to an airtight container and freeze.

While the sorbet may be used in 3-4 hours, it has a better texture when it has had a day or two in the freezer. Makes 4-5 cups sorbet.

FILBERT COOKIES

Whether they are called filberts or hazelnuts, the flavor is special.

1¼ cups toasted filberts, finely ground*
¼ cup light corn syrup
2 tablespoons brandy
1 cup butter, room temperature
1 cup sugar
1 egg, room temperature
1 teaspoon vanilla extract
1 cup whole wheat pastry flour**
1 cup white flour
½ teaspoon baking soda
½ teaspoon salt

Combine the ground nuts, corn syrup, and brandy. Let stand 20 minutes.

Cream the butter and sugar. Add the vanilla and egg. Combine the flours, soda, and salt. Add to the creamed mixture. Add the ground nut mixture and combine well.

Form into 1″ balls and place 2″ apart on an ungreased baking sheet. Bake in a preheated 350° oven about 12-15 minutes. Makes 5 dozen cookies.

To toast filberts: Place on a baking sheet and toast in a 350° oven about 20 minutes. Turn onto a towel and rub to remove most of the skin (some always remains). When grinding filberts, keep a close watch, as there is a fine line between fine-ground filberts and filbert butter!

**Do not use regular whole wheat flour. *If you do not have whole wheat pastry flour on hand, use white flour as a substitute.*

GINGERBREAD CAKE with CARAMELIZED PEARS

This could also be named the "Goldilocks Cake." There were versions that were "too hard" and others that were "too soft" before we were happy with the final result—which is "just right"! It has a delicate texture and exactly the right amount of spice. The "gingered" whipped cream and the caramelized pears add a perfect finish.

3 cups flour
1 teaspoon baking soda
1 teaspoon cinnamon
1 teaspoon powdered ginger
½ teaspoon allspice
½ teaspoon cloves
½ teaspoon salt
½ cup pear puree (about 1 small ripe pear)
½ cup buttermilk
1 cup butter, room temperature
1 cup packed brown sugar
¾ cup molasses
3 large eggs
Caramelized Pears (recipe follows)
½ cup whipping cream
1 tablespoon sugar
2 teaspoons minced crystallized ginger

Grease and flour a 10″ bundt pan. Set aside. Sift the flour, baking soda, cinnamon, powdered ginger, allspice, cloves, and salt. Set aside.

Combine the pear puree and buttermilk. Set aside.

Cream the butter and brown sugar. Add the molasses. Add the eggs one at a time, making sure the first is incorporated before adding the next (do not be alarmed if the batter looks curdled at this point). Alternately add the sifted dry ingredients and the pear mixture to the batter, scraping down the sides of the mixing bowl to make sure everything is incorporated. Pour into the prepared bundt pan. Bake in the center of a preheated 350° oven about 50 minutes—until a toothpick inserted in the center comes out clean and the cake pulls away from the sides of the pan. (While the cake is baking, prepare the caramelized pears.) Remove the cake from the oven. Cool in the pan for 10 minutes. Remove from the bundt pan and set on a cooling rack. The cake may be served warm or at room temperature.

Whip the cream with the 1 tablespoon sugar, until soft peaks form. Fold in the crystallized ginger. Slice the cake and arrange on individual serving plates. Top each slice with whipped cream and caramelized pears. Serves 12-14.

CARAMELIZED PEARS

3 tablespoons butter
4 ripe pears, peeled, cored, and cut into
    ¼″ slices
¾ cup sugar

Melt the butter in a large, heavy-bottomed skillet. When the butter is sizzling, add the sliced pears. Toss the pears to coat them with the butter. Sprinkle the sugar over the pears and stir. Cook, stirring gently, over medium to medium-high heat until the pears are caramelized and tender, about 5 minutes. Remove from the heat and cool to room temperature.

Menus and Northwest Wine Selections

Over the years at the Steamboat Inn, Sharon and Pat have developed some favorite menu combinations for their evening meals. Because certain dishes complemented each other well, they have gradually become familiar partners on the evening menus. And, of course, the most popular menus increase in popularity because returning guests continue to request them.

Even so, there is no such thing as a "set" menu at the Steamboat Inn. Pat and Sharon continually adjust their menus, factoring in requests from guests, seasonal availability of fresh foods, and their desire to feature variety in the meals. Some dishes just naturally seem to bring out the best in each other: Baked eggplant, for instance, enhances a well-prepared leg of lamb in subtle ways. If an entrée is deemed somewhat "soft" in texture, it may dictate a crisp side dish or a heavier bread in the menu for balance.

Color balance in menu planning is often overlooked and sometimes difficult to achieve. Sharon and Pat use red peppers, cherry tomatoes, pimentos, carrots, and red cabbage—along with other colorful vegetables—as garnishes to add the proper contrasts and color blendings on a plate. Even so, the question "What can we add for color?" is often repeated at their Monday menu-planning sessions.

Matching the right dessert with an almost-completed menu often takes some puzzling, too. The cooks take care to never follow a cream sauce or other heavy entrée with a dessert that's overly rich. Chocolate may follow beef or chicken, but never lamb. Fish dishes are best followed by a crisp citrus dessert, to cleanse the palate. Keep those contrasting colors and textures in mind with dessert, as well!

Even though most cooks at home will never face the juggling act that Pat and Sharon confront with their weekly menus, the Steamboat Inn system works in the home, too. It's a good idea to keep records of the menu combinations you've served to guests, including notes on how the meal was received. If you entertain frequently, your records will remind you what was served to your guests last time around. They are certain to appreciate sampling a variety of menus from your kitchen.

So take note of the favorite Fisherman's Dinner combinations that follow and prepare to let your creative juices flow.

1

Seasoned Lamb and Feta in Phyllo

Carrot Almond Salad on Mixed Greens

Barbecued Boneless Chicken Breast

Mushroom and Parsley Pilaf

Cauliflower, Snow Pea, and Black Mushroom Stir-Fry

Sesame-Garlic Rolls

Walnut Cake with Walnut Praline Mousse

2

Jalapeño Ham Puffs

Spinach Salad with Pear Vinaigrette

Chicken Breast with Orange Thyme Butter Sauce

Orzo

Stir-Fried Vegetables

Walnut-Onion Bread

Citrus Gâteau with Bavarian Cream

3

Gingered Shrimp Toasts with Fresh Fruit

Napa Cabbage and Filbert Salad

Cornish Hens

Fruited Wild Rice Stuffing

Steamed Broccoli

Parsley-Chive Bread

Lemon-Blueberry Crêpes

4

Cherry Tomatoes and Snow Peas with Seasoned Cheese

Broccoli and Flank Steak Salad

Grilled Salmon Fillets

Walnut Rice

Steamed Asparagus

Whole Wheat Dill Bread

Walnut Strawberry Roulade

5

Spinach and Mushroom Frittatas

Herbed Walnut Salad

Scallops in Feta Cream Sauce

Jalapeño Pasta

Asparagus, Snow Pea, and Mushroom Stir-Fry

Basil and Sun-Dried Tomato Bread

Pear-Cranberry Sorbet and Filbert Cookies

6

Spicy Chicken Wings

Fresh Tomato and Spinach Salad with Basil Vinaigrette

Red Snapper with Jalapeño Lime Marinade

Green Chili and Corn Soufflé

Broccoli with Ginger-Sesame Butter

Herb-Cheese Bread

Rhubarb Upside-Down Cake

7

Curried Zucchini Soup

Baked Eggplant with Curried Tomato Sauce

Garlic Baked Leg of Lamb

Herbed Parmesan Potatoes

Sautéed Carrots with Raspberry Vinegar

Steamed Broccoli

Parsley-Chive Bread

Pear Tart

8

Jalapeño and Dry Jack Wontons

Crisp Red Apples

Sesame Asparagus

Barbecued Lamb Chops

Rosemary-Blue Cheese Potatoes

Broccoli with Roma Tomatoes and Jicama

Herbed Sourdough Bread

Apple-Blackberry Crisp

9

Stuffed Mushrooms

Red Cabbage with Walnuts and Blue Cheese

on Mixed Greens

Seasoned Lamb in Phyllo

Herbed Carrot Ring

Stir-Fried Vegetables

Herb Biscuits

Fresh Peaches with Raspberry Puree

10

Herbed Chicken Strips with Fresh Fruit

Tortellini and Mixed Greens

Barbecued Flank Steak

Soy-Sesame Potatoes

Green Bean and Mushroom Stir-Fry

Whole Wheat Seed Bread

Chocolate Crêpe Gâteau

11

Curried Pork Turnovers

Spinach Salad

Barbecued Beef Tenderloin

Cheesy Grated Potatoes

Brussel Sprouts and Carrots with Rosemary

Cracked Wheat Sourdough Bread

Chocolate Mousse Tart

12

Chèvre Tart

Spinach, Bacon, and Jicama Salad

Marinated Pork Tenderloin

with Glazed Onions

Wild and Brown Rice Pilaf

Zucchini and Three-Pepper Stir-Fry

Sesame Bread

Gingerbread Cake with Carmelized Pears

Wine and Food in America

by Stephen J. Cary and David J. Anderson

The last ten years in America have seen a renaissance in quality dining. Every aspect of good food, from its conception to the selection of basic ingredients, preparation, and service is enjoying a revival of interest. Food lovers eagerly analyze the interesting new offerings from innovative restaurants and chefs. A vital part of this new food awareness is the burgeoning American wine industry. To complement food with wine by mixing, matching, and seeking combinations that work well is a pleasure enjoyed by many food and wine lovers.

Wine plays an integral role in fine dining. It stimulates the appetite, aids digestion, and sparks a good time. The myriad flavors of wines and their ability to enhance the flavors of foods make wine a valuable addition to a good meal. Over time, wine has developed its own complex, often vague descriptive language. It is confusing—occasionally overwhelming—to even the most serious food lover. Therefore, the guidelines that follow will help in selecting the right wine to complement specific dishes.

Formerly, there was just one rule for wine selection: white wine with fish, red wine with meat. But as the awareness and interest in fine dining has blossomed, revised guidelines have developed. Indeed, the exuberance of the burgeoning American wine scene in the 1970s was nothing short of rebellious, creating an "anything goes" atmosphere. We began drinking any kind of wine with any kind of food. Many innovative, even startling, food and wine combinations resulted.

The thoughtful and creative efforts of food and wine lovers throughout America continue to develop new guidelines—more complex, yet more accurate—that take into account far more than just the flavors of foods and wines. Understanding the makeup of food wines is the key to great food-wine matches. While a wine's flavor influences choice, we now look for the wine's structure, its texture and feel. The goal is to find wines that keep the palate fresh and counterbalance the flavors of the meal—food and wine flavors that together produce a sum greater than the parts. The subtle *differences* in flavors and textures of various foods and wines, not their similarities, are what create the harmony in a successful combination.

Wines are often defined in abstract terms that do not describe their compatibility with food. A good food wine should have enough acid to be crisp and refreshing, cleansing the palate of oils and sauces and inviting another bite of food. Many wines which seem a little sour or sharp when drunk alone are often perfect with a meal. Wines should have enjoyable flavors of their own; they should not be too soft nor too easy. In sum, a well-balanced wine should have no single dominating component; rather, a tapestry of woven flavors—acids, oak, alcohol, and sugar—is most desirable.

The Northwest enjoys climatic conditions conducive to the production of wines that are dependable food complements. Oregon wines, for example, made from grapes grown in a cool region, preserve the fresh, crisp feel so important in a fine table wine. With some varieties naturally better suited for the dining table, their subtle complexities harmonize with a tremendous variety of foods. For Oregon, the best example is Pinot Noir, made from the great red grape of Burgundy. Because of this grape's delicate, yet complex flavor, it produces a wine that is both subtle and rich. Oregon Pinot Noir matches beautifully with a broad range of foods from grilled fish to spring lamb, from veal tenderloin to summer salads. It is, most often, the single best choice.

White Riesling, grown in the Northwest's cool climate, produces nearly dry wines with low alcohol content and an attractive acid crispness. This variety, sometimes called Johannisberg Riesling, is pleasant for just sipping or as an accompaniment to poached salmon, poultry, fresh fruits, and salads. Northwest Rieslings have re-awakened Americans to this delightful white wine variety.

Gewürztraminer, when harvested with the proper ripeness in the Northwest, produces a luscious, spicy white wine. Its fragrance and robust flavors complement a wide range of foods from smoked fish to Cajun and Oriental dishes.

Other Northwest wine varieties that enhance many food creations include dry Chenin Blanc, Sauvignon Blanc, and a new variety to America, Oregon Pinot Gris.

As American cuisine moves towards lighter foods with a subtle complexity of flavors, our preference in wines has shifted in the same way. Finding the right combinations of food and wine is fun, educational, and limitless. The wines of the Northwest, especially Oregon, offer many well-suited choices.

Also worth noting are several popular wines that have relatively limited food affinity. Chardonnay, while it is the darling of the American wine scene, is not the perfect match for many foods. We find two general styles in Chardonnay: The buttery forward, "fat," and soft Chardonnay is enjoyable as a beverage while the higher acid, more delicately fruited Chardonnay, with light oak tones (or no oak at all), enhances many poultry dishes and light meats, medium sauces, vegetable dishes, and light entrées. Cabernet Sauvignon and Merlot are two popular red wine varieties that do well with a limited number of dishes. These full-bodied wines have a strong, single-dimensional flavor and tannin, best suited for heartier meals.

Rather than attempt to clarify every descriptive term, we have taken another tack in making the following recommendations. Both climate and variety play critical roles in determining the nature of a wine and its best use. Cool climates, such as those of Burgundy, Alsace, Germany, and Oregon, produce elegant, subtle, complex, crisp wines. By contrast, warm climates, found in Australia, Spain, and most of California, produce full, soft, simple wines. And intermediate climates, including Washington State and California's Carneros Region and south coast counties, often produce wines that blend the characteristics of both warm and cool regions.

While some varieties, such as Chardonnay, grow well in any grape-producing region, the resulting wines will be very different. Other varieties, Pinot Noir in particular, only produce top quality wines in quite restrictive climatic conditions. We find that choosing by variety alone is not enough. Our experience leads us to consider the nature or texture of the wine first when matching it with food. After we have found the right degree of weight and crispness desired in the wine, we then look for flavors that harmonize with the food. We are not looking for wines that taste "just like" the food. We do not want either the food or the wine to dominate; rather, in the equation of fine dining, both factors must be identified—but especially, enjoyed.

In general, we favor the wines from cooler climates when choosing for the table, finding the crisp, fresh feel of wines from such regions ideal with a majority of foods.

The following is a list of specific recommendations for the twelve dinner menus in this book. Normally, there is more than one wine that will successfully complement any dish. In our suggestions, we have usually listed several options, including European wines from appropriate climates. The Oregon wines we have listed offer especially good value, but, should it prove difficult to find the Oregon wines, we have also included other alternate American and European varieties.

WINE SUGGESTIONS

MENU	COURSE	REGION	STYLE	TYPE
1	1st	CC	DW (light)	Macon, French Chablis, Light Oak Oregon Chardonnay
	2nd	CC	LR	Nouveau, Light Oregon PN, Beaujolais
	Dessert	–	–	Just Coffee
2	1st	CC/IC	ODW/LR	Oregon or Alsace WR, California South Coast Counties JR/ Beaujolais, Oregon Light PN
	2nd	CC/IC	SDW/LR	Oregon or Alsace GT, Light Carneros PN, Oregon Light PN, Beaujolais, Oregon-California SB
	Dessert	CC	D	Oregon Raspberry
3	1st	CC/IC	ODW/ SDW	Mosel, California South Coast Counties JR, Oregon WR, Oregon or Alsace GT
	2nd	WC	DW	Napa, Sonoma CH
	Dessert	AC	SWD/SPK	LH WR or JR/ Sparkling
4	1st	CC	SDW	Oregon or Alsace GT
	2nd	CC/IC	LR	Oregon PN, Burgundy, Carneros PN
	Dessert	AC	SWD/SPK	LH WR or JR/ Sparkling
5	1st	CC/IC	DW	Dry CD, Dry WR, SB
	2nd	CC/IC	ODW	Vouvray, Oregon, Washington WR
	Dessert	–	–	Just Coffee
6	1st	CC/IC	SDW	GT, Dry Muscat, SB
	2nd	CC/IC	LR	Oregon PN, Beaujolais
	Dessert	WC	SWD	LH Muscat
7	1st	CC/IC	SCW	GT, SB
	2nd	CC/IC	FR	Full-bodied Oregon PN, Carneros PN, Burgundy, Medium California ZN
	Dessert	IC	SWD	True Sauterne, LH Muscat
8	1st	IC/WC	LR/SDW	Lighter Red Bordeaux or Claret Style American CS/SB
	2nd	CC/IC	FR	Full-bodied Oregon PN/American ME
	Dessert	CC	D	Oregon Blackberry
9	1st	CC/IC	SDW	Dry GT or Fino Sherry
	2nd	AC	LR	Light Spicy Reds, i.e. Valpolicella, Rioja, Beaujolais, Claret-type California ZN
	Dessert	CC/IC	D/SPK	Oregon Raspberry or Sweet Sparkling (Asti Spumanti)
10	1st	CC/IC	SPK	Brut Sparkling
	2nd	IC/WC	FR	Red Bordeaux, American CS
	Dessert	–	–	Just Coffee, or Dinner Red
11	1st	CC/AC	SDW	CC GT/AC SB (White Bordeaux/American SB)
	2nd	CC/IC	FR	Full-bodied Oregon or Carneros PN/ Medium-bodied CS or Bordeaux
	Dessert	–	–	Just Coffee, or Dinner Red
12	1st	CC	LR	Beaujolais, Oregon Nouveau PN
	2nd	CC	FR	Burgundy, Full Oregon PN
	Dessert	AC	SWD	LH WR, LH Muscat

REGION

AC/All climates
CC/Cool climate
IC/Intermediate climate
WC/Warm climate

STYLE

D /Dessert
DW /Dry White
FR /Full-bodied Red
LR /Light Red
ODW/Oregon Dry White
SDW/Spicy Dry White
SPK/Sparkling
SWD/Sweet White Dessert

TYPE

CB/Chenin Blanc
CH/Chardonnay
CS/Cabernet Sauvignon
GT/Gewürztraminer
LH/Late Harvest
ME/Merlot
MU/Muscat
PG/Pinot Gris
PN/Pinot Noir
SB/Sauvignon Blanc
WR/JR/White Riesling/ Johannisberg Riesling
ZN/Zinfandel

Aside from providing you with specific definitions and explanations, we feel the best advice we can offer is: Take the time to read a recipe thoroughly. Once you have read and understood a recipe, you should assemble the necessary ingredients and *only then* begin preparation. It can be very frustrating—sometimes disastrous—to be partially through a recipe and realize you have overlooked a necessary ingredient or a critical step in the preparation. The more relaxed you are and the less you worry, the easier—and more fun—cooking will be!

Try to use your own best judgment when you encounter a new term, such as "until the sauce heavily coats a spoon." The first time through a new recipe is always the most difficult. If a recipe appeals to you but you realize you are missing an ingredient, try to think of an acceptable substitution you may have on hand. The flexible and innovative person has two of the "Ingredients" necessary to becoming a good cook.

Although we have tested and retested these recipes, preparing them in your own kitchen will be different from preparing them in ours. The particular ingredients may vary from area to area, or a skill level will differ. It may take several tries to perfect a given recipe or technique. Another important thing to keep in mind is the "personality" of individual ovens and their accuracy. There is also a difference in cooking with gas or electricity. Use the times stated and work in any necessary adjustments for your own kitchen. *Bon appétit!*

BALSAMIC VINEGAR: An Italian, sweet/sour, wine-based vinegar that has undergone long aging in a variety of wooden barrels—each a different wood. Balsamic vinegar may be found in specialty markets and may be used in a variety of ways—in salads or meat marinades, or on freshly steamed vegetables.

CHÈVRE (Goat Cheese): A versatile cheese that may be incorporated easily into any menu course. It may be purchased either fresh or aged from your local deli or the cheese section in your local grocery store.

CHILI GARLIC SAUCE: This is a very spicy chili sauce. We often use this in place of dried chilies, as it is in paste form and provides a fuller flavor. *Tuong OT Toi VietNam* is the brand we use.

CHINESE DRIED BLACK MUSHROOMS: A dried and wrinkled, dark-colored mushroom with an underside of fawn-colored gills. These mushrooms lend a very distinctive accent when used with vegetables or in soups. They are available in oriental markets or in the specialty section of grocery stores.

COUSCOUS (Ground Semolina): Quick-cooking couscous is a form that is readily available from natural foods stores, either in bulk or box form. Couscous can be prepared in a matter of minutes and may be served either hot or cold. It has a nice texture and its relatively bland flavor lends itself to an infinite variety of seasonings.

EGGS: Our recipes always call for large eggs. To assure better texture and volume in your recipes, eggs should be removed from the refrigerator one-half hour prior to assembling your recipe to allow them to warm to room temperature.

FETA CHEESE: A salty, Greek goat cheese found in delis or in the cheese section of your local grocery store.

GINGER IN BRINE: Sliced into thin strips and preserved in red brine, this ginger can be stored indefinitely under refrigeration. We use it primarily as a garnish, although it has a crisp, ginger flavor.

GINGER, CRYSTALLIZED: Ginger that has been sliced, dried, and sugared. Available in oriental markets or along the specialty aisle of some grocery stores. We use it as a flavoring in desserts. The *Roland®* brand is widely available.

GLOSSARY

GINGER, FRESH: Available in the produce section of most grocery stores, it should be rock-hard with a smooth, tan outer skin. When sliced, it should have a gold inner flesh and, sometimes, a ring of green at the outer edge. To store, peel and place in a jar with a tight-fitting lid. Cover with dry sherry and refrigerate. It will hold indefinitely and the "gingered sherry" is a wonderful flavoring for stir-fries and soups.

HOT OIL: A hot, spicy oil made from infusing spicy red peppers into either vegetable or sesame oil. It is also called chili oil, hot pepper oil, or red oil. We use *China Bowl Hot Oil*.

HERBS: Fresh herbs are our first choice, but when necessary, we prefer to use crushed rather than powdered herbs. If you must use powdered, you will have to decrease the amounts in our recipes.

NUT OILS (i.e. Walnut and Hazelnut): These delicate nut oils are best used as flavorings, as they tend to break down under high heat. We use them extensively in salad dressings. When opened, the oil should have a fresh, nutmeat odor. After opening, store the oil in an airtight container and place in a cool, dark place or under refrigeration. Nut oils may be found in specialty stores and some grocery stores.

OYSTER SAUCE: When used sparingly, this sauce adds a subtle background accent to fresh, crisp vegetables. The *Panda* brand of *Lee Kum Kee* is the one we most often find available.

PHYLLO (FILO OR FILLO): A paper-thin pastry used to encase fillings for appetizers, entrées, and desserts, phyllo is available fresh or frozen from delis or some grocery stores. If purchased frozen, let it thaw in the refrigerator for two days before using. Phyllo will dry out rapidly if left exposed, so keep the dough covered with a towel when working with it.

PICO PICA®. One of the many Mexican-style hot sauces available. We have not explored the market in depth but have found *PICO PICA®* to lend a hearty spiciness without being harsh.

RICE VINEGAR: A white to golden vinegar that is more full-flavored and less harsh than most distilled vinegars. The brand we use most often is the green labeled *Marukan®*.

RICE WINE: A sweetened Japanese cooking wine. AJI-MIRIN is the brand we use in salads and marinades. Sake may be used as a substitute.

SESAME OIL: The sesame oils we work with are Oriental. The best-flavored ones, made with toasted sesame seeds, produce a golden brown oil, rich in aroma and flavor. Sesame oil tends to burn easily and is best used as a seasoning.

STOCKS: Generally, we use hearty, homemade, unsalted stocks. Be very careful when reducing commercial "broths" as they may be very salty and the salt intensifies as the broth reduces. *Swansons®* is now offering a lightly salted broth and there may be others available in your area.

SUN-DRIED TOMATOES: Available in some specialty stores, sun-dried tomatoes packed in seasoned oil are generally expensive, but it is relatively easy to make your own. Both *Sunset* and *Bon Appétit* (August 1984) have featured articles on drying tomatoes.

YEAST: We use active dry yeast (1 tablespoon = 1 package). The warm water called for should be between 105° and 115°. If substituting compressed (cake) yeast, use one 3/5-ounce cake per tablespoon of active dry yeast and reduce the water temperature to 80°-90°.

ZEST: Gratings of the rind of citrus fruits (orange, lemon, etc.). Use only the colored, outer layer, as the white, inner layer is bitter. Tightly wrapped, zest keeps well in the freezer.

INDEX

ACKNOWLEDGEMENTS

There are several people we would like to thank who helped us in so many diverse ways with this book. It's true—we couldn't have done it without them! To Dan Callaghan, our thanks for your special friendship and for sharing your love affair with the North Umpqua through your scenic photographs. Your never-fail support and enthusiasm has been a real boost to us over the course of this book. And Mark Hoy—thanks for your "faith" in the book and all the research hours spent before we had any commitment that any of us would ever see our work in print. The historical text and sensitive interpretation of the "Steamboat Experience" could not have been conveyed any better.

The food photographs are the work of E. J. Carr of New York City. Thanks, Ed, for leaving the Big Apple behind and venturing out west to share your keen eye and skill as a photographer, not to mention your patience with two inexperienced "food stylists."

Peter Coyne just happened to be at the Inn the evening our publishers were visiting. That evening, Peter was coaxed into reading some of his poetry. The next thing we knew, the book had a poetic element added to it. Thank you, Peter, for the well-chosen words that accompany Dan's photographs and the many other poems you have shared with us over the years.

Judy and John Waller enthusiastically applied their illustrating expertise to each introductory page and proved that a picture is worth a thousand words by sketching the process of boning a chicken. Our thanks to you both.

Stephen Cary of Cary Oregon Wines has always been generous about sharing his years of experience and his knowledge of wine (and wine itself!). Thanks, Stephen, for your participation in the food and wine article, the wine suggestions, and for all the wonderful guests you have brought to Steamboat over the years.

Stephen introduced us to David Anderson, now the Marketing Director at Knudsen Winery and co-author of the food and wine article. When we thanked David recently, his reply was "no problem—it's always easy to rewrite Stephen's words." Well, thanks again, David. Modesty is so becoming to you.

We decided the day before our manuscript deadline that this book needed a map to reference the historical text. Our friend David Harris responded to our call. David, thanks for your last-minute efforts and for sharing your skill as an artist through the clear, concise map.

We also would like to acknowledge the invaluable contributions made behind the scenes. Thanks to Bob Jagelski of Pro Photo in Portland who generously loaned Ed Carr the lighting equipment needed for the food photographs. Barbara Fontaine devoted many late evenings to help edit the galleys. Thanks, Barb. Special thanks to our staff—for working around us in a small kitchen and tasting version after version of the same recipe. Our evening crew helped test some of the dishes, often working from half-finished instructions. Thanks for your comments and critique.

This book may never have gotten off the ground if Glen Sorum hadn't given us the name of a friend of a friend, Doug Pfeiffer. Our thanks to Glen for giving us Doug's name. Doug is Vice President and General Manager of Graphic Arts Center Publishing. Doug Pfeiffer spent college summers on the North Umpqua and shared many meals at Steamboat Inn. Thanks, Doug, for holding onto your memories and giving our manuscript more than a cursory look.

This book's readibility and recipe consistency is largely due to the combined efforts of Shelley Bedell-Stiles and Jean Andrews. Our special thanks to you, Jean, for your editorial skills, patience, and willingness to educate us to the workings of the publishing world.

Last, but not least, thanks to Keith and Jim, our husbands, who were ready with encouraging words, enthusiastic participation, and a willingness to taste, critique, and help with the stacks of dishes.

Patricia Lee and Sharon Van Loan